MW01482221

The Wild Woman's Guide to Social Media

by Mazarine Treyz

A hands-on, how-to guide to marketing your business in 15 minutes a day using blogging, Twitter, and more!

ISBN: 978-1-4675-1281-7

Library of Congress Cataloging-in-Publication Data:
Treyz, Mazarine.
The Wild Woman's Guide to Social Media: A hands-on, how-to guide to marketing your business in 15 minutes a day using blogging, Twitter, and more!/ Mazarine Treyz

ISBN: 978-1-4675-1281-7
1.Internet marketing. 2. Social Media. 3. Online Social Networks. 4. Small Business. 4. Nonprofits

Printed in the United States of America
First Printing: October 2012

Cover Design & Image by Sarah Perry of http://snperrydesign.com
Cover Production by Danielle Bardgette of http://www.daniellebardgette.com/

Bulk Sales
Chattaranga Press offers excellent discounts on this book when ordered in quantity for bulk purchases or special sales. For more information, please contact info@wildsocialmedia.com

Dedicated to Steve Havelka, the kindest person I have ever met.

Thank you to my grandparents, Betty and Peter Treyz, for helping me understand how to explain social media more clearly.

Thank you to my friend Jacob Feinberg, for helping me create the first worksheets of this book.

Thank you to my friend Pamela Grow, for sharing so many opportunities and for being so giving and kind!

Thank you to Sarah Perry and Danielle Bardgette for making my book look beautiful.

Thank you to my blog readers, e-newsletter subscribers, and Twitter followers, for helping me feel like my voice is being heard.

Thank you for reading!

Table of Contents

Why Wild?

Wild means scrappy and tough, willing to try anything, and always keep learning. I've worked for myself and for nonprofits for years-I know how to make do, stretch the budget as far as it will go.

With this book, you can do wild social media tactics for yourself, AND:

- Start from nothing and build your business
- Find and keep a job based on your online reputation
- Figure out what you should focus on in social media, get the biggest bang for your buck, and save time.

I haven't done social media for a big corporation. I've done it for small businesses, small nonprofits, and for myself. Let's face it, when your livelihood is on the line, you work harder, you find tactics that work for a small company, tactics that a multinational corporation may not even think of!

Listen to someone who has been where you are. I started with no contacts, no website, no Twitter, and no one who cared what I had to say. If you have no resources and no road map, this book will take you step by step into building a name for yourself and your business.

My successes with social media include:

- Teaching and selling lots of technical hands-on webinars and workshops.
- Writing and selling physical books and ebooks all over the world.
- Learning how to do a successful launch with partners.
- Teaching and selling lots of art classes.
- Getting hired to do social media for others in the worst economic downturn the US has ever seen.
- Making a living through teaching and writing because of my social media relationships.
- Creating an online community of partners and fans including 21,000 monthly readers and 3,000 Twitter followers.

I encourage you to get wild! Wild Social Media helps us get the word out, not just to build our businesses or nonprofits, but to create tribes. To create movements. Wild Social Media means being switched on all the time, engaged, aware, and curious about everything. Wild Social Media means never sitting back and saying, "I know enough."

About Mazarine Treyz

Born and lived as variously as possible.

I've lived in a one room apartment in Seoul Korea, in a shack on the beach in Maine, a baby orphanage in Indonesia, a student efficiency room in York, England, a trailer in Arkansas, a geodesic dome in Portland, Oregon, a grand house in Westchester, NY, and a little house in Austin, Texas.

How do you live wild? Live without dead time.

I've been blogging since 1999. Ever since September 11th 2001 in New York, I realized I wanted to help people, but I did not know how. I started researching, and traveling, this led to fundraising, and that led to becoming involved in the nonprofit tech community and writing my first book, The Wild Woman's Guide to Fundraising, and that led to me selling my book all over the world, teaching workshops and webinars, which led to this book.

When I'm not teaching, I'm biking around Portland, Oregon, with the most beautiful person in the world, writing, making encaustic art, and hiking.

Connect with me on Twitter, I'm @wildwomanfund
Get free stuff at http://wildsocialmedia.com/i-bought-the-book

(Author photo by Mazarine Treyz, 2012)

Why Should You Read This Book?

- **In 2010,** there were 1.8 billion Internet users and a world population of 6.7 billion.
- **In 2020,** it is estimated that there will be five billion Internet users! *

This is worth TRILLIONS of Dollars to your business. You need to be there.

Content, aka what you know, and how you get it out into the world via blog posts, tweets, updates, videos, etc, is what the first part of this book will help you create. The second part will help you with Connection and Community.

Why should you build community? Because you will:

1. Build your network before you need it.
2. Share your story to help people connect to you.
3. Allow people to add their own pieces of the greater story. Leave lots of room for positive mutation. People feel ownership when they contribute.
4. Make it easy, fun, and meaningful to share the message with friends.
5. Make folks feel proud & important, like they're a part of a larger community working on common goals.
6. Reward and celebrate your heroes.

The third part of this book is worksheets to help you take action ASAP. No excuses! Just getting out there now!

There are more people than ever online. It's harder and harder to get heard in the noise! The good news is, with the techniques you will learn in this book, you CAN be heard, and this book will not only help you do this, but help you get more customers and more cash too!

Ready to jump in?

---

* http://www.intac.net/the-internet-in-2020/ Predictions from Intac.

Preface: Their Rules and How We're Gonna Break 'Em

You know the rules. The old rules.

Press Releases
Billboards
Radio ads
Bus ads
Street Banners
Get in people's faces constantly.
Buy your membership to the Better Business Bureau

That's the old reality.

You can still have all of that stuff, but now if people want to find you

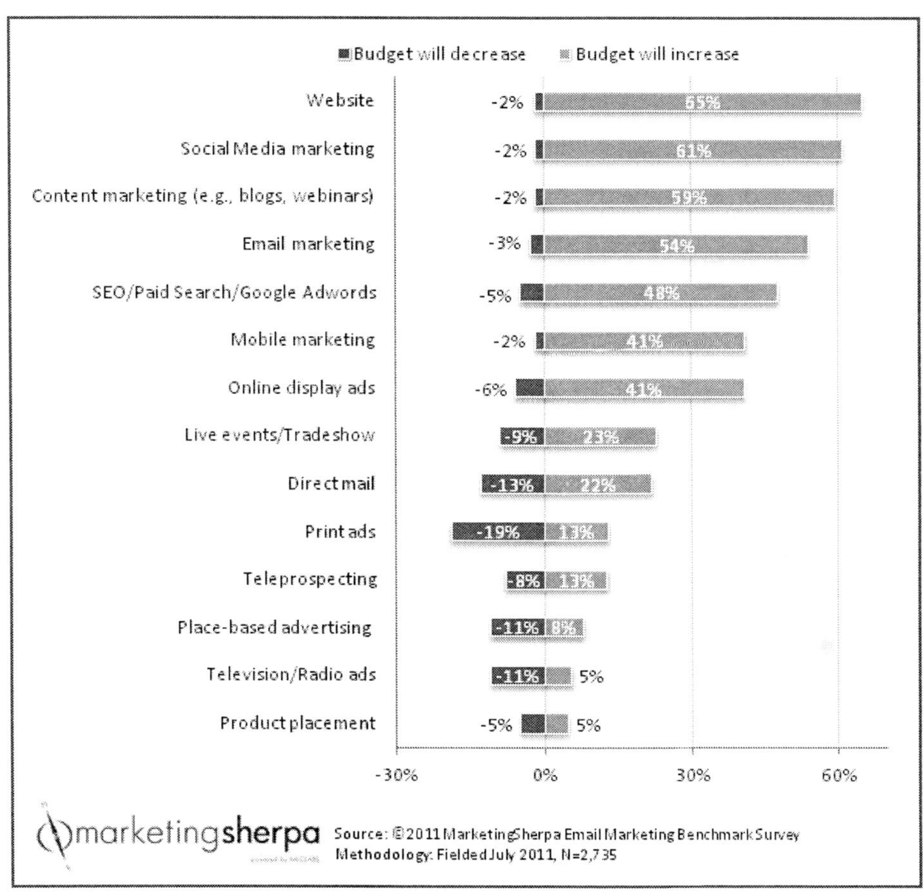

they'll search for you online first. The new reality is that Social media/Digital Marketing are poised to take over.

People are opting out of marketing messages more and more. And big companies are paying attention to what works.

Proof? Here's a Marketing Sherpa Email Benchmark Survey (data from July 2011).

You can see here of the thousands of people surveyed by Marketing Sherpa, they found people were planning on spending much more money on their websites, on their email, Search, and Social media, and planning on spending much less money on print and broadcast ads.

The reason they are doing this is because social media marketing and advertising works. Digital marketing is emerging as one of the best ways to connect with potential customers and clients.

You don't have to take Marketing Sherpa's word for it. Test these theories for yourself. I would advocate surveying your current customers and seeing how they found out about you. Direct mail and broadcast ads may still work for your customer base. Just don't let that be all that you do.

Social Media is like wrapping customer service, marketing and sales into one big ball, and running with it.

Want to play?

Chapter 1: When the unthinkable happens

When I was fired in 2009, I was incredibly scared, yet exhilarated. I had hated my job, and yet I was stuck in the middle of the swiftest and most decimating downturn our country had ever seen. On top of that, I was in one of the worst cities in America to be unemployed in, aside from Detroit. I was in Portland, Oregon, with a city motto of, "The City That Works." This city had a 25% unofficial unemployment rate, and people wryly joked that Portland was "The City That Doesn't Work." Thanks to excellent marketing, and a cheap cost of living, people moved there in droves from 1995 to 2009, which kept wages low and unemployment high, making it the self-employment capital of America. Mostly in food carts, as far as I could see.

My low-paying nonprofit jobs and high county taxes had left me with no savings. Even though I was a successful fundraiser, raising more with events and grants than had ever been received before, I had given all of my hard work to nonprofits who didn't value me. Without my title, I was suddenly a nobody. I didn't know what I was going to do. My family had never understood why I wanted to change the world, why I had to go off to the west coast and deny their continuous advice to become a dentist. They didn't have much sympathy, and I knew I couldn't go back.

So I fired off resumes every week, went to networking events, asked around in my social circles, and even with my interviewing skills, after seven or eight interviews over the course of four months, and hearing they had decided not to hire anyone at all, or hire a consultant instead, I started to see the pattern. Manufacturing had left Portland for cheaper shores, and with the manufacturers, a lot of money. There were lots of darkened and papered up storefronts. No one could afford to buy. Goodwill was bursting with newly desperate people clutching third-hand shoes. It became a low-paid service economy, like much of America. Nonprofits didn't have money to hire because their own donors didn't have as much money. I had to abandon this dying economy.

So I got a little... wild. I decided I was going to blog and speak my truth. I decided it was better to speak my truth than stay silent. If I never worked again in the nonprofit field, I would accept with the consequences.

I got out to Texas, which had a slightly better economy. As soon as I laid eyes on sunny Austin on October 5th, 2009, I loved it.

When you move to a new place, the problem becomes, "How do I get started in a new city where I have no network at all?" I started to read about internet marketing. I bought a domain, created my first Wordpress site, and started to blog professionally in November, 2009. Since 1999 I had been writing on the internet in one form or another, and had a personal blog, but never thought of blogging as something to support me.

Then I started to read. I realized I had the tools and the time to create a reputation no one could take from me. I started to write. I started to blog about nonprofit management and fundraising 5 days a week in February 2010. My stats skyrocketed to 7,000 readers per month. In April 2010, I started my own newsletter. I got 100 subscribers quickly, and worked hard on my social media marketing.

In 2010, when I published my book, *The Wild Woman's Guide to Fundraising*, it was called one of the top ten nonprofit books of 2010 by a famous author and CEO of Zoetica, Beth Kanter. I sold books all over the world, from Finland to Tasmania, from England to New York City.

Suddenly, I was getting calls to speak, to get syndicated, to endorse products, and people were asking me to fundraise for them, and to teach them how to do what I was doing. In 2011 I was named as a City of Austin vendor for Social Media Training. It's a far cry from being an unemployed nonprofit nobody living on spaghetti and scouring craigslist for free wood to heat the apartment.

Even in the worst economic downturn our country has ever seen, I've managed to help myself and others make money. I've made the most of this new digital marketing reality.

I did it by getting wild.

I don't mean wild by taking stupid risks or taking drugs. I mean the wildness of standing up for what you believe in. When you face the truths about your field, head on, when you're strong enough to say what everyone else is thinking.

Do you want to have success in any economy? Do you want to Get Wild, use social media, and speak your truth too?

Come and join me on this journey, you'll be surprised and delighted where it takes you!

Chapter 2: We are all media companies?

People are often not aware of their social media reputation until they Google themselves or their business and think, “What is this junk, and how do I get rid of it?” or “I'm not even ON here” or “That famous person with my name is everywhere. How will anyone ever know about me?”

The good news is, you CAN get found online, and this book will not only help you do this, but help you get more customers and more cash too!

Where have we come from?

Let's have a little history
When the internet first came out, we call that Web 1.0. Web 1.0 says, Here’s my content! People took their brochures and made their websites say the same thing as their brochures. And visitors couldn't engage with the website. They couldn't comment, they couldn't see what was new. Likewise website owners couldn't see as easily who was looking at their website, they couldn't get the word out about their website unless they were part of a link exchange, or web-ring. The web

What’s Web 1.0?

- Brochure websites
- Hierarchy of connections.
- One-way flow of information.
- OBSCURITY

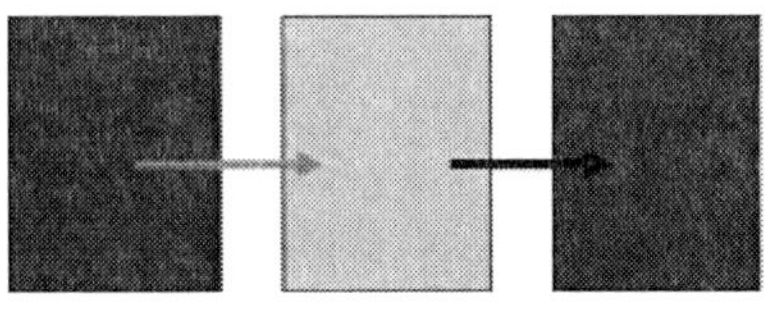

was a much more static and unchanging place. Now we are moving through Web 2.0, which is about facilitating conversations.

Who are you when you're online?
How comfortable are you on the internet? Do you create? Do you comment? Listen? Collect?

On the web, are you a *Creator*? -of a blog, a website, a video, a podcast, etc?

Are you a *Critic*? (do you often comment on videos, blogs, websites?)

Are you a *Collector*? (do you collect articles on topics that interest you?)

Are you a *Joiner*? (do you like to join groups related to your interests on the internet?)

Are you a *Spectator*? (do you just like to watch?)

Or are you *Inactive*? (do you not get this internet thing at all?)

In web 2.0, you need to be able to listen, to respond, and create community where everyone shares.

So, does your web strategy:
Help you listen?
Does it start conversations?
Does it let users share?
Do your strategies integrate? (i.e. Having a coherent voice across platforms?)

What's Web 2.0?

- Dynamic websites
- People connecting via all kinds of social networking sites.
- Free exchange of information.
- TRANSPARENCY

To be successful in this niche, you must become a creator and a critic.
You need to consistently create useful content, and be aware and commenting on important articles and blogs, tweeting and having conversations and opinions on what you read.

The reason that it's important to listen, have conversations and comment is because you want to be aware of what other people in your niche are saying. You need to learn who else is out there, who you can count as an ally, who could promote your work, whose work you could promote, and who you could learn from.

How do you help people trust you enough to buy from you?

"Every Company is a Media Company (EC=MC)"
-Tom Foremski, journalist, http://siliconvalleywatch.com

Every Company Is a Media Company is the most important business transformation of our times because every company is affected. It is also a massive business opportunity for so many businesses."
-Tom Foremski*

What Foremski means is, whatever product or service you sell, whatever kind of nonprofit work you do, you are also a media company. You must be active online in monitoring your reputation and providing free valuable information to people.

Foremski has recently revised his EC=MC to include the idea that everyone is a media company, but no one is very good at it. Because people are not good at being media companies, they're not sure what will work. So they just throw money at things. People may be trying to sell you space in the yellow pages, in their newspaper, on their TV or radio station, even on their websites. Wouldn't it be helpful if you knew straight off which sources of information people trust more than any other? Where should you be focusing your efforts? Where should you be advertising? Let me save you some money and clear up this confusion.

When you look at the chart on the following page from the Nielsen company, you'll see the majority of people trust recommendations from other people they know first, and then they trust consumer opinions posted online. This means if you want your customers to trust you, you need to generate referrals and recommendations. No matter what kind of business you have, if you have a website, you can start providing value through your company blog that will lead people to make recommendations to your site and to your company.

---

* http://www.siliconvalleywatcher.com/mt/archives/2010/04/new_site_every.php

Trust in Advertising — April 2012

(% of global online consumers)

	Trust completely/ somewhat	Don't trust much/At all
Recommendations from people I know	92%	8%
Consumer opinions online	70%	30%
Editorial content like newspaper articles	58%	42%
Branded websites	58%	42%
Emails I signed up for	50%	50%
Ads on TV	47%	53%
Brand Sponsorships	47%	53%
Ads in magazines	47%	53%
Billboards & outdoor ads	47%	53%
Ads in newspapers	46%	54%
Ads on the radio	42%	58%
Ads before movies	41%	59%
TV show product placements	40%	60%
Ads in search engine results	40%	60%
Online video ads	36%	64%
Ads on social networks	36%	64%
Online banner ads	33%	67%
Display ads on mobile devices	33%	67%
Text ads on mobile phones	29%	71%

(from Nielsen)

Generating recommendations offline may include investing in customer service, going to networking events, and having an open house. Remember, people don't trust TV, Newspaper ads, Magazine ads, billboards, radio ads or even online ads as much as they used to. So when you think about where to spend your money, invest creating free value for your potential customers. Then that will help you listen, and get people to trust you.

Chapter 3: Why You'll Get Stuck

Pick the one that applies currently.

1. You haven't done this before.
2. You'll self sabotage and procrastinate.
3. Your self talk will be all "No, You can't!"
4. You'll think of lots of things you urgently need to do instead.
5. You'll have no community of people encouraging you.
6. You'll get overwhelmed! Too much! Too fast!
7. You'll get impatient for results before you should be expecting any.
8. Your family and friends don't understand why you're doing this.
9. You're afraid of failure.
10. You're afraid of success.
11. You're afraid you'll never be able to stay on top of all of the new developments, even if you do succeed.
12. You don't want to write.
13. You can't think of anything to write about.
14. You get jealous of someone who has "made it."

Let's address these one by one.

1. **You've never done this before?**
   So, there's a lot you haven't done before! Why not ask yourself how you can stretch yourself each day, how you can make your life more significant?

2. **You procrastinate?**
   It's common in the beginning! Just notice that you're doing it, stand up, take a break, go for a walk, come back refreshed.

3. **Your self talk is negative?**
   Consider that the majority of people who get on Twitter tweet

once and then stop. If you tweet twice, you are different than the majority of people! You can and WILL be different. You've bought this book. You've already invested in your future. You're ahead of most people.

4. **You have a lot to do?**
Then go and do it! Come back to this, squeeze it in even in 15 minutes a day!

5. **You have no community?**
Come and say hi to me on email or twitter (@wildwomanfund) and I will introduce you to people I know. We will share our successes, encourage you to take action, and help you keep learning.

6. **Overwhelmed?**
Too much, too fast? Feeling overwhelmed? It's okay! You can't keep on top of everything and you shouldn't try to. Create space for breathing and quiet time each day. Everything will become easier to deal with.

7. **You're impatient for results?**
What you're doing right now is building towards results. Just know that you will get results if you build relationships with people. Clients and customers will refer you to friends, family, and associates. Watch your stats climb each week and each month. Don't expect too much in the first 6 months. You'll find your number of visits going up, your number of pages going up, your numbers of followers and connections going up too!

8. **Your family and friends don't understand?**
Nobody in my family reads my blog. It's probably not something they will really get. That's okay though. They don't have to understand. You can point them to the success stories of other people. This is the new marketing reality. It will be there, whether they believe in it or not. You can tell them, hey, Google is the new phone book and encyclopedia, and I need to be where people can find me.

9. **You're afraid to fail?**
Of course! Everyone is. The definition of courage is being scared to death, and saddling up anyway. So acknowledge your fear. And move forward in spite of it. Even the smallest web presence will

be a little movement. And better than no move at all.

10. **You're afraid of success?**
    What if you succeed? Wow! You'll have to keep building on your success, keep writing, keep rolling out products, keep tweeting, and that's a lot of work! Of course you're afraid you might succeed. But when you get successful, you can hire people to help you continue to build your momentum. Even part time people can edit your products, and help you write your e-newsletter, and more! No one ever succeeds in a vacuum. All success depends on other people in some ways. So ask for help.

11. See above.

12. **You don't want to write?**
    You don't consider yourself a writer? You don't think you have anything to say. There's no way around it, in order to succeed in this field, you are going to need to write, a lot. You don't have to embrace the title of writer, but that is what you'll be doing, day in and day out, whether you're writing blog posts, commenting on other blogs, posting to Twitter or interviewing someone.

13. **You're jealous of someone else's success?**
    Well, acknowledging it is good! You're inspired by their example, and you CAN succeed. If you think they've said everything, you're wrong. There are lots of things that you can say. You are different, and you'll say things a different way. Now that you have a picture of what success looks like, start to retweet, mention, and comment on their blog. You can start to build a relationship with them.

To sum up, my advice is: You may be scared. You may procrastinate. You may hem and haw and wish this whole thing would just go away.

Well, welcome to reality. Saddle up anyway.

And What To Do About It

1. **Just know that it's hard.** Social Media is work. You need to do it every day.
2. **Be contrarian.** This goes against what we are taught, but being contrary can actually make people like you even more.
3. **Tough love.** You are going to be alone for much of this process. You need to keep motivating yourself. No excuses for not following through.
4. **Be willing to listen, to hear the truth and answer.** When your customers or clients have criticisms, you have to be strong enough to face them and see if there is any truth, answer publicly, and be brave enough to say, "I'm sorry" and "I don't know" and "Their product is better. We're working on ours."
5. **Choose things that align with your values.** You may think you can compromise your values a little bit here and a little bit there, but in the end, you lose yourself.
6. **You have something of value to give to the world.** Always do your best to give it to them. And the more best you're capable of, the more you should do.

1. It IS hard. Social Media is work.
You need to do it every day. People who tell you they will make you an overnight millionaire with the internet are lying. Just run in the opposite direction as fast as you can. You have to know you can do it, but it takes work! Serious work! Hard work! Mental work! Showing up work!

It's not all kittens and rainbows, but that doesn't mean you can't have fun! You can insert humor or quirkiness into your blog posts. You can acknowledge universal truths, that people in your field struggle to accept. To keep yourself awake and motivated, remember you are finally free to say the things you held your tongue about all of these years.

Simon Sinek says, ***"The goal is not simply to "work hard, play***

hard." The goal is to make your work and your play indistinguishable."

I write because I truly love writing, and I need to do it. You don't have to stop there though. You can be a podcast host. A video person. An interviewer. A person who has conversations. A researcher, reporter or role model. You need to be a creator. And that can be hard. But hard compared to what? Hard compared to wasting thousands on advertising that people tune out, making your business less and less money? Or hard compared to just changing your habits enough to show people the fascinating truth about your field?

2. Be contrarian.
This goes against what we are taught, but being contrary can actually make people like you even more. In creating content for your website, in leaving opinions and facts on other people's blogs, your contrariness will generate controversy, which will get people to come to your site, sign up for your updates and buy from you.

So, that formula is: Contrariness → Controversy → Visitors → Sign-ups → Customers

3. Tough love.
You are going to be alone for much of this process. You need to keep motivating yourself. No excuses for not following through.

So what does tough love mean? Well, you know it's hard. That's why I wrote this book, to make it easier on you. But that means now you have no excuses for not following through.

4. Be willing to listen, to hear the truth and answer.
When your customers or clients have criticisms, you have to be strong enough to face them and see if there is any truth, answer publicly, and be brave enough to say, "I'm sorry" and "I don't know." When you have the courage to be vulnerable, to admit your mistakes, you help people trust you.

When you get out there online, you need to know people will message you and try to interact with you. If you respond, you will have started to grow a loyal customer. If you don't respond, you've missed an opportunity to engage with your current or future customer.

You might hear from disgruntled customers. And you might hear from satisfied ones too. You can keep a list on the side of your website for compliments that people give you. People will be kind, and will interact, and you need to give them that chance. Potential customers believe what other people say about you a lot more than what you say about you.

Give the happy people a place on your site! And see if you can turn unhappy customers into your advocates.

5. Choose things that align with your values.
You may think about compromising your values online. Someone will offer you some money and if you just have a bit of moral flexibility, you could make money with them. But this would be a terrible idea.

For example, say you are a pro-choice feminist. You are starting your speaking career and a person approaches you, out of the blue, to speak at his conference. You Google his name and find out that he's anti-choice, gives money to pregnancy resource centers, and thinks that wives should obey their husbands because of the bible. So, should you do business with this person? No. Not in a million years. It will make you miserable. He is not who you are trying to help. He represents everything you stand against.

So first, articulate your values. What are your non-negotiable things? Who do you want to partner with? Who do you want as your customer or client? Is there anyone you would NEVER partner with? Anyone you would NOT want as a customer? How far are you willing to be flexible?

And where do you STOP being flexible?

If you've got a social conscience, and you want to “make a difference” with your business, articulate your vision for that a little more. HOW will you “make a difference?” Specifically. Which industries or causes are you specifically interested in? Which align with your values? If you get known for your corporate social responsibility to a particular cause, this will help people who do align with your values target you and come to you, and help people who have nothing to do with your vision of philanthropy stay away. It helps stop wasting everyone's time.

6. You have something of value to give to the world.
You got into business because you knew that you had something of

value to offer the world, something people would be willing to pay for.

Think of blogging like being in business. You have something of value to offer, and it's up to you to SHOW and TELL people that your value is there, day in and day out. If you can become a trusted resource for your niche, you will find people flock to you at speaking engagements, classes, workshops, customers, clients, and more. This will happen because you have made yourself available, shown what you know, and are able to articulate how you help others in your niche.

If you are an expert in several areas, consider how you can monetize each of these areas. You can be simultaneously, an expert in fly-fishing, interior decoration, AND bookbinding, for example.

When you think of what you're good at, also think about what people on your team or in your circle are good at. If there's someone you've always wanted to talk shop with, but never had an excuse, now is the time! You have a publishing platform, you have a place to hold the knowledge that can benefit many people. It is so worth it.

Chapter 4: Decide who to be online & who to reach

What is it? The idea of building up your reputation online has to start with this first step. What do you want your reputation to be? In what industry? How will you differentiate yourself from others in the space?	**When to do it:** Figuring out good keywords should be a recurring part of your marketing process, every 3-6 months.
What you'll need: 3 things that make you different Knowing your strengths and weaknesses An idea of what people are willing to pay you for. Sense of what you want to offer.	**What to do:** Figure out what you want to offer Figure out who your customers are Figure out where they are Think about your potential customer's pains, goals, and agendas when brainstorming keywords for your business. *Do your keyword worksheets in the back of the book.*

Getting Clear

- Who do you want to be online?
- Who is your audience?
- What do they want?
- How are you different from your competitors?
- Define what you want to offer, and define success: # of sales, # of customers, traffic, public perception

Step 1: Who do you want to be online?

People have this schizophrenia thing when they start blogging or having websites online. How much do you conceal? How much do you reveal? How much can you say without going over some sort of invisible line? What will you say to build your reputation? What would you NEVER say? Think about your ethics and values as well as your comfort zone. One thing I've learned is that it can be good to get in there and write about what you can't stop thinking about. Don't blog about your personal life, except incidentally. Keep it separate and keep it professional.

Step 2: Figure out who your customers are and what they want.

This is actually trickier than it sounds. A lot has to happen between the time a person thinks, "I have no problem" to "I need to buy what you have NOW!"

Start by doing market research. Pick up the phone and call your potential or previous customers. Ask them what their major issues are right now. What problems do they have? What are their goals?

First, what is the problem they're trying to solve? That will often tell you where they are and who they are. What are their pains, goals, and agendas? And finally, how do you help them?

Customer Problem	Customer Goals	Customer Pain	Customer Agenda	Your Solution

Step 3: Create and Disrupt!
Your new content must get out there consistently. To quote John Jantsch, author of the New York times bestseller, *Duct Tape Marketing* and *The Referral Engine*, new content will drive your business.

So, where do you get your content?
Read as much as you can. Look at; Books. Twitter. Other people's blogs. Newspaper articles. Magazines. Radio shows. Podcasts. Your own employees and their institutional knowledge about your company. Setting up a series of interviews is a wonderful way to get people engaged in your company. Show the real people, but show the way you

do business too. Your trust factor will rise.

How do you disrupt with your content?
You know you can do it. Think of all of the sacred cows in your industry. Which ones have you been wanting to tip? Think of the way things are done, the way information is exchanged in your industry. Use the traditional channels, go where people are, but also think about: how could you get the information out a different way? If people read trade magazines, could you make a podcast? If people listen to podcasts, could you make an e-newsletter?

Step 4: Use Multiple Channels
What does this mean? You can use Twitter, Facebook, LinkedIn, Wordpress, YouTube, Flickr, podcasts and other channels to get your information out there.

Step 5: Ask for truth and answer in your social media efforts, AND Step 6: Engage in conversation beyond your comfort zones
Go where you're afraid to go. Answer that angry customer. Talk with your competitors. Get your CSR reps to give their stories. The level of transparency on the web can often be shocking, but that doesn't mean that it's bad. In fact, it's good. The more open you are, the more people are interested in your life, and how you do business, and most importantly, WHY you do it the way you do it, instead of the way other people do it.

Step 7: Keep actively learning. Thank your teachers.
Alvin Toffler, a futurist, quotes a conversation with Herbert Gerjuoy, and says:

"The new education must teach the individual how to classify and reclassify information, how to evaluate its veracity, how to change categories when necessary, how to move from the concrete to the abstract and back, how to look at problems from a new direction — how to teach himself. Tomorrow's illiterate will not be the man who can't read; he will be the man who has not learned how to learn."[*]

How you can apply this to your own case is that on the web you can never rest on your laurels. You need to be constantly learning, because there's a lot of competition. You can ride the wave, or you can stand on

* http://en.wikipedia.org/wiki/Alvin_Toffler

the shore. But remember, if you looked in a phonebook last year, you were one of an increasing minority. You need to be where your people are. They aren't looking at the phonebook anymore. So where are they? Depending on the industry, where they are is always changing. See if you can follow some people who are ahead of the curve, and ask for their opinions and advice on what the next big thing is for your industry.

Step 8: Build Your Community.

This entire book will show you how to build an online community. Offline, that's up to you.

Step 9: Get help when you need it!

This could just as easily be Step 1. And every step after that. One of the best ways to learn is by asking for help! Admitting you don't know, and getting to a place of understanding is the only way to get good at anything.

So, to quote Quincy Jones, check your ego at the door and let's get down to work!

Chapter 4.1: What are Keywords?

What is a keyword?

Look at the word, keyword. It's a word that unlocks the search engine and lets you get found. People search with keywords. You need to put the right keywords in your content to get the right visitors to your website. For example, if you sell tires in Boulder, Colorado, your keywords include: “flat tire, new tire, 80301, boulder co.”

Why are keywords and keyword rich articles so important?

The point of keywords is to get the right number of the right kinds of people to visit your site, specifically, the people who need what you have, and to get them to take action, aka buy your products or services.

Keywords help people find you specifically. You have to hone in on what people are looking for, so you must choose what words you want them to associate with you.

Choose keywords for example, that describe:

- Your character, values
- Your products, services
- Your customers, their demographic, their industry, their job title
- Your customers’ pain, agenda, problem.
- Your geographic location
- Your industry
- Your vendors, subcontractors, partners

When you want to differentiate yourself from what others are doing, putting in highly specific keywords helps you stand out more to potential clients.

Top Tip: The more relevant keywords you can think of for yourself, the better off you'll be in search results. Go all out. Think of as many keywords as you can. And you don't have to do it on your own.

The best keywords are the words that have high relevance to your market, high traffic and low competition. How can you find out what has high traffic and low competition? Use the tools below.

How to find good keywords:

- Use the Google Keyword tool. http://adwords.google.com/select/KeywordToolExternal Think of questions and phrases that you've searched for in your niche. Remember the phrase, and surround it with quotes when you search for it. When you search for your exact phrase in Google, how many search results come up? This will show you how common this search is, and how many people are interested in this particular phrase. When you divide the traffic by the competition, that's how many pages you'll have to beat to get to the top. Look for fewer than 1,000 competing pages for your keywords. Researching keywords with low competition that are relevant to your market will pay off.
- You can also use the search string: "allintitle: Keyword1+keyword2" for example allintitle: fundraising+women and remember to use misspellings of your keywords as well, such as "fudnraising" or "fund-rising".
- You can also use MarketSamurai.com or Wordtracker.com to research keywords.
- Put your keywords into Google and look at the ads that pop up around this search. What words are THEY using?

For example, specific keywords for my fundraising consulting business are: "Grant research, event coordinator, how to get sponsorships, fundraising ideas, how do I find grants, best nonprofit blog."

These keywords should go in the Header section (or H1 tags) on your website to make you most visible to search engines. Your keywords should also go into your image descriptions, tags, and image titles, as well as your blog post tags and page tags, and your video tags. This helps you get found not just with Google, but with Google image search, or a video search.

Do you see how I had tons of keywords and phrases above? The idea is to get geographically specific, as well as use phrases that often come up in search results. Use industry specific jargon too, like the investment banker jargon below.

More examples: if you're an investment banker, the words "investment banker" should be in your keywords, but also "stockbroker" "portfolio" "affluent clients" "Private equity fund manager" "trusted advisor" "post merger integration" "private equity" "institutional investor" "senior lending" etc.

To come up with good keywords, you need to know your audience. And more than that. You need to know more than what their job is. You need to know what their Problems, Goals, Pain, and Agenda are.

I've made you this handy diagram so you can do just that!

Customer Problem	Customer Goal	Customer Agenda	Customer Pain	Your Solution

Once you realize what words people are searching for when they have a problem that you can help solve, you'll be much more likely to get good search traffic of a specific subsection of people who would want to buy from you. You'll see an example below of how you can fill out your diagram. You're a gluten-free bakery. Your ideal customer? Someone with a gluten allergy.

Problem	**Goal**	**Agenda**	**Pain**	**Solution**
So many baked goods have gluten, I can't find anything to eat!	Find something delicious & quick for birthday party.	I don't have time to cook for myself, or gluten-free baking is too difficult.	If I eat gluten, I'll have a severe reaction. I can't risk any contamination.	Our delicious gluten-free baked cakes, baked in a dedicated facility!

If you're a company that publishes books, you need to be looking at the search terms people are using when they need information inside these books, not just the book titles.

Must Know

- Keywords help people find you
- Researching keywords can help you get higher Google search

rankings

- Putting as many tags as you can in your content helps people find you

Must Do

- Do market research calls to your current or potential customers
- Find out your customer's pains, goals, agendas and problems
- Research using the Google Keyword Tool

Chapter 4.2: Keywords and Search Engine Optimization

SEO stands for Search Engine Optimization. This means that you supposedly optimize your website so that search engines will put your website in the first 3 pages of search results about your niche.

In the early days of Search Engine Optimization (SEO), people thought that good SEO came from using a lot of keywords in your article, your tags, and your blog article title. In this way, they reasoned, they could game the system and come up first in search results.

Old efforts to do SEO include something called "Keyword Stuffing" where people would say the word they wanted to rank for over and over again in the blog post. If the internet is our phonebook, then this should help more people find you, right? Well no.

This led to a lot of fake blogs coming up first in search results, making Google look bad. This led to Google changing its algorithms so that people could not "game" the system this way. People keep trying to find new ways to get on the front page of Google for random keywords, and Google keeps coming up with ways to fix that issue. So trying to game the system is going to lead to failure. There's no way you can keep up with what Google is doing. It's just going to lead to wasted effort.

Do you like wasting effort? Me neither.

Loading up your articles with keywords that you want to rank for is not going to work as well as offering valuable content, day after day, about people's pain, agenda, and rewards in your industry. This is why I'm telling you that the best way to do Search Engine Optimization is to just create compelling content, over and over again. This is called Content Marketing. This means people start to know, like, and trust you, not because you have managed to out-spend everyone else, but because you actually have useful information that can help them.

According to the book *Convert!* by Ben Hunt, the best SEO is no SEO at all. If you keep creating relevant, original, useful content that you are passionate about, you will stand out in a world full of people just going through the motions. And THAT is powerful. That will take people back to your site again and again.

I've seen this happen with my own website. I've written articles for over two years about the fundraising world, and people have responded with spontaneous compliments, sharing my e-newsletter and articles with others, and buying my products. How I keep going is by writing every day, writing about how I feel, what I think, articulating my values or experience in fundraising.

This is the hard way, but it's also the easy way, because you can study to scam the system, and maybe rank on page 2 of Google for a week, but in a week Google can change their search algorithms and then all of your web pages will be buried on page 20 of the search results again.

As of this writing, October 2012, Google is privileging search results that;

- Have a lot of backlinks from .gov and .edu, (Trustworthy folks!)
- Are old but still regularly updated, and
- Include Google properties such as YouTube and Android Apps or Google Play. (Which is a wonderful reason to have your own App)
- Are from people with their own Google ads. So if you buy Google ads, you'll get up higher in search results.

Google is also privileging websites that are called the exact keywords people are searching for. This means if you own a website called "HowToGetSponsorships.com" and people type in "How to Get Sponsorships," then your website will come up higher in search results, maybe on page 2 or 3 instead of page 30 of the search results.

So remember, SEO is a nice thought, but it's not going to make your business successful in the long run.

Must Know

- Connect with your customers' pain and they'll want to share your content
- When people share your content, it leads to incoming links,

which leads to better SEO.

- Trying to game the system is not going to work.

Must Do

- Think laterally to uncover alternative needs: Not just "car detailing" but "learn car detailing" for example.
- Ask yourself, is there more than one market?
- List as many problems as you can, and state your solution to those problems.

End of Chapter Questions: What did you learn?

What are keywords?
What are YOUR keywords?
Where do you put keywords?

Chapter 5: Start to Listen to Your Customers

What is it? Listening online is how you manage your reputation, anticipate what your customers or donors want, and stay on top of the latest resources for your field.	**When to do it:** Listening should be an ongoing process for your business.
What you'll need: Listening tools include: Netvibes.com Google alerts for your keywords SurveyMonkey Email survey to your current customers RSS feed for your company and leader's name.	**What to do:** Ask your potential customers where they are active. Ask people to retweet, mention, and comment on your posts on Twitter, LinkedIn, your blog, and Facebook page. Set up accounts on SproutSocial, PeopleBrowsr, and use Tweetreach.

Where are your current customers or donors?

- Are they in forums?
- Are they on Twitter?
- Are they on Facebook?

How do you know? Did you survey them? Once you survey the people who currently give you money, you'll figure out where you need to be.

You can't expect instant results. And you have to give yourself room to fail. With this in mind, what would constitute success for you?

For example:

- For the first three months, success could be number of people reached.
- For the next six months, success could be number of people at your store increasing, or less shopping cart abandonment in your online store, or more people at your open house.
- For the two months after that, it could be increased number of sales.

You need to measure what is happening, and you need to analyze how people are mentioning you.

Social media is about conversation, sharing, and engagement, not just PR.

How can you start to see your own progress? Build a baseline. Where are you now? How many people are mentioning you? How many people are following you? Once you have a baseline, you can start to measure your progress. Put your current followers, mentions, and other things you want to track in a spreadsheet.

How can you monitor social media community talk, and start to listen?

- Use Twitter chats to start to listen. Use Tweetreach to see who has the greatest influence and amplification of the Twitter chat.
- Use Edgerankchecker for Facebook to listen to what's happening there.
- Listen in LinkedIn Groups related to your field.
- Use AllTop.com to research top blogs in your field.
- Do a simple Google search with your keywords and see who comes up first. Is it people just spamming the system? People with good things to say? This can show you what people are saying and not saying.
- Set up a Google alert (if you don't know how, go to http://google.com/alerts to learn) for your name, business name, website, and relevant keywords for your industry.

After you listen, take action.

Now that you know where people are active and what they are saying about you, how can you take action to respond?

- If people are saying negative things about you, take it offline as quickly as possible, so you can respond clearly to their concerns.
- If people are saying positive things about you, ask them if you can highlight their compliments on your website.
- If no one is talking about you yet, make a list of 10 blogs you want to comment on regularly.
- Participate in a Twitter chat or post on an active forum.
- Give a talk.
- Call a potential client that you found online.
- Join a LinkedIn group, introduce yourself, talk about your expertise, and link to your site.

You want to track and see which of your strategies is working. Keep a spreadsheet of everything you do each week, and then look at your Google analytics stats for that day to see what worked best.

	Mon Method	Tues Method	Weds Method	Thurs Method	Friday Method
Results	Comment on three to ten blogs	Participate in a chat / post on a forum	Give a free webinar/ give a talk	Call up a potential client/	Comment on a LinkedIn group
Uniques/ pages					
Tweetreach					
Sentiment analysis					
Clickthroughs on your links					
Influencers tweeted your message					
Sales					

How can you connect with influencers who can drive LOTS more traffic to your site? People find your website by accident, so how can you keep touching them?

1. Maybe they sign up for your newsletter.
2. You can see if they have a website, leave a comment on their blog.
3. Follow them on Twitter.
4. Comment again on their blog
5. Tell a friend on Twitter that the blogger is neat. Connect someone

directly with them.
6. Then ask them to comment on your post.

Goals for Blogger relationships
Get bloggers to retweet you
Get them to write blog posts
Get talked about with the bloggers telling friends
Get people to follow you, buy things from you, visit your site.

To engage your community

- Respond to them. @ mention them on Twitter. Email them. Call them.
- Put your top influencers in lists so you can track them more easily.
- Participate in Twitter chats with them.

When you start to measure engagement, what is important? You can't measure your bottom line yet.

According to Forrester research, they like to measure: "Involvement, Interaction, Intimacy, and Influence"*

Involvement:
How involved are you in the conversation? Say hello and ask questions on a Twitter chat, in a forum post, in a comment stream on an industry blog.

Interaction:
You could make a goal to increase the volume of buzz or link amplification (getting people to share your posts or comment on your post) by 10% in your blog posts and comments within 3 months of engaging the blogging community.

Intimacy:
Can you speak on your social media platforms like you're talking to an old friend? Do people find your writing meaningful for their own situations?

Influence:
Social media doesn't require you to see a strategy through to the end

* *The Forrester Sequence, Marketing's New Key Metric, engagement, by Brian Haven, Forrester, 2007.*

because social media marketing is constantly changing. This means you can throw out what isn't working, and keep what is.

When you do all of the above, your social media influence will rise and more people will visit your site, sign up for your newsletter, and buy your stuff. When you do marketing and communications, these are often the only things you can measure with certainty. It's hard to track exact marketing efforts back to actual sales. Just keep this in mind as you start this journey, and we'll look at metrics tools to help you figure out which of your marketing activities are the most valuable.

Must Know

- The best way to keep track of what people say about you online is to set up your listening dashboard.
- Establish baseline metrics as you start to listen, so you have something to track as you go.

Must Do

- Survey your list. Are they on Twitter? Facebook? Just email?
- If you don't have a list, ask people in your industry what their experience is.

Chapter 6: Tools You Need to Build a Community of Buyers

By now you know you need to be providing content.

It would be a mistake not to engage in social media at all, but it ALSO would be a mistake to try to do everything. So what kind of content do you want to provide?

There are so many options, as you can see from the picture below, that you could easily get overwhelmed with everywhere to be, and everything that you don't know.

The neat thing is, once you read the next few chapters, I'll teach you, step by step, how to blog, how to comment, how to write e-newsletters and which skills you need to have (or hire out) to do these things effectively. Your website is your brand hub. It's also the place you want to draw people back to, so they can buy your products or services. Below you'll see a few different platforms to establish a presence online. We aren't going to be talking about every single platform in this diagram, just the ones that I feel are most beneficial for beginning to market your business or nonprofit online.

We're not going to talk about YouTube, for example, because it's difficult to make a professional-quality video, and if you don't have good production values, you're not going to inspire confidence in your potential customer. We're not going to talk about podcasting, because again, it's difficult to have a professional quality podcast with lots of listeners. We're not going to talk about photo-sharing because I have never gotten any sales from Flickr, and unless you're a photographer, it's not the best way to get the word out about what you do. Your customers are not hanging out there.

We'll talk mobile, insofar as you know it's important to have a mobile version of your website. Apps are also useful.

In the next part of the book we'll talk mainly about content marketing through social networking, email marketing, micro blogging and publishing.

Chapter 6.1: Converting Visits to Sales, Step by Step

What is it? People tend to look in certain places on your website for answers to their questions. This chapter will help you set up your website to get your visitors to take the action you want them to take.	**When to do it** When you first set up your website, and then whenever you want to increase your sales, or at the start of a new campaign.
What do you need? Tynt.com Optomizely.com VisualWebsiteOptimizer.com e-newsletter stats tracking	**What to do?** Watch your stats Do A/B testing, aka changing where things are on your site to see what gets people to buy

The first tool you need is a website. If you already have a website, is it as effective in getting you sales as you'd like it to be? If not, read on.

Whenever people go online, they are looking for something, whether it's an answer to a question, or simply a way to waste time.

If you know that people come to your website searching for answers, you want to make sure that your solutions to their problems are front and center. This way they'll stay on your website longer, and consider you a resource. This can lead you to how to set up your website pages and content.

Let's start with how to get people finding your website with the right content. Arrange your website to create a ladder of engagement*.

* The concept of the Ladder of Engagement comes from a book called *Convert* by Ben Hunt. I have created this diagram based on his idea.

What does this ladder look like?

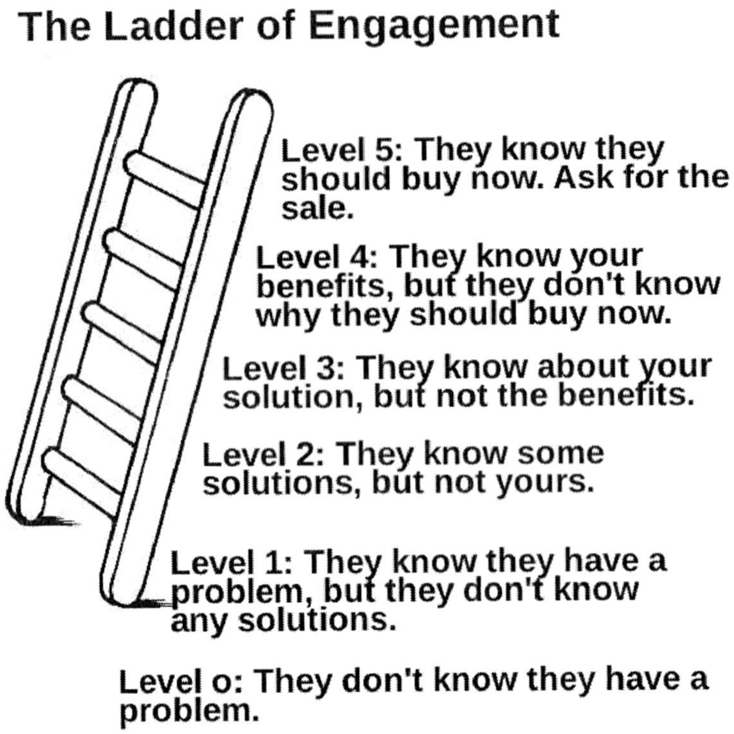

Level 0. Customer doesn't know they have a problem.

Level 1. Customer knows they have a problem, but doesn't know what to do!

Level 2. Customer knows they have a problem, there might be solutions but they don't know about your solution.

The Ladder of Engagement

Level 5: They know they should buy now. Ask for the sale.

Level 4: They know your benefits, but they don't know why they should buy now.

Level 3: They know about your solution, but not the benefits.

Level 2: They know some solutions, but not yours.

Level 1: They know they have a problem, but they don't know any solutions.

Level 0: They don't know they have a problem.

Level 3. They know about your solution, but why is it better?

Level 4. They know your solution is good, but why should they buy NOW?

Level 5. Your solution is the best! They will buy it now.

Think about your customer. Ask yourself:

- What is their current level of awareness?
- What are they looking for right now?
- What are they open to at this point?
- What will get their attention?
- What next step can you invite them to take?
- What do you need to convince them of for the next step to make sense?[**]

** Hunt, Ben. *Convert*! Pg 51-53. Wiley, 2011.

Create specialized pages that speak to each of these points, for all of the steps on the ladder. For example, let's take a tax accountant in Los Angeles, California.

Level 0: They don't have a problem, as far as they know. This is the education level. Don't make a page for this type of person. They are too difficult to reach. Focusing on this level takes a MASSIVE amount of effort, and only works if you know there's a large untapped market.

Level 1: They know they have a problem. So match their problem terms with your pages. If you are a tax accountant, for example, you can call this page or blog post “Tax Headaches!” or “10 Quickbook tips” or “What are some overlooked deductions?” or “How can you finish your taxes FAST?” This is where your keyword research comes in handy. For pages focusing on this level, discuss the issue in general, acknowledge their pain, and suggest solutions that may exist. At the bottom of the page, link to the next steps in your ladder.

Level 2: Aware of some solutions to their problem (not your solution) Create more articles that match more specific terms: “Turbo Tax, H&R Block, Los Angeles, Tax accountant, Extra time to file, Federal Taxes LA”. You can come at the issue from multiple angles, and mention alternatives. You can even talk about your competition, such as TurboTax, and explain the pros and cons of going with different solutions. At the end of the page you talk about your solution, and link to the next step on the ladder.

Level 3: Aware of your solution (but not the benefits)
You can create more articles based around questions around your company. Like “What kind of deductions can I get?” or “How quick is the turnaround?” This is where you should put the benefits, the evidence that what you sell really works.

Level 4: Aware of your benefits (but not convinced)
In these articles or pages on your website, you want to give them a mental picture of what life will be like once they have bought your product or service. Speak to their agendas and their goals. This is where you put your testimonials from happy clients who got big tax returns, press clippings, and thank you notes from happy customers.

Level 5: Convinced and ready to buy

How do you close the sale? You must ask for the sale. You need to be clear, strong, and repeat the ask. Give them appropriate timing and placement. That means make a button that says What the person wants to Get, to Do, to Know or Where They Want to Go. And make these buttons noticeable. Make them big elements, with space around them. You can even make them a bright color not used on the rest of the page. Maybe use 3-D effects like gradients or shadows around the buttons (*Note: this is easy for non-programmers to do with the Wordpress Headway Theme*). Make sure this is the only place they can go when they get there.

To sum up, you must have a target audience with specific problems in order to get the most from this method. The better you know your audience, the better you will be able to write to their pain and connect with them and start to convince them to give you their money.

What does this look like as a website?

Look at a screenshot from one of my websites, http://GetSponsorships.org. I've labeled the steps for you.

Get Sponsorships

You can get BIG sponsorships for your nonprofit event!

Level 1 Level 2 Level 3 Level 4 Level 5

Home | What are Sponsorships? | How to Get Sponsors | How Can We Help You? | Get Sponsors Now | Contact

Sign up and you get

When you're organizing an event, what 3 things guarantee success?

Posted on July 12, 2012 by admin • 0 Comments

In the last several years, I've raised hundreds of thousands with events. For example, with one event I organized in 2007, I raised $75,000 with a gala and auction event that had raised $65,000

This is just one way you can set up your website to address people on different parts of the ladder.

Designing your website for conversions

What are conversions? A conversion is whenever a website user takes the action that you want, whether it's buying your goods or services, donating to you, signing up for your e-newsletter, sharing your links with friends, and more. The diagram below is called the Google Heat Map. It shows where people are most likely to look for useful information on your website.

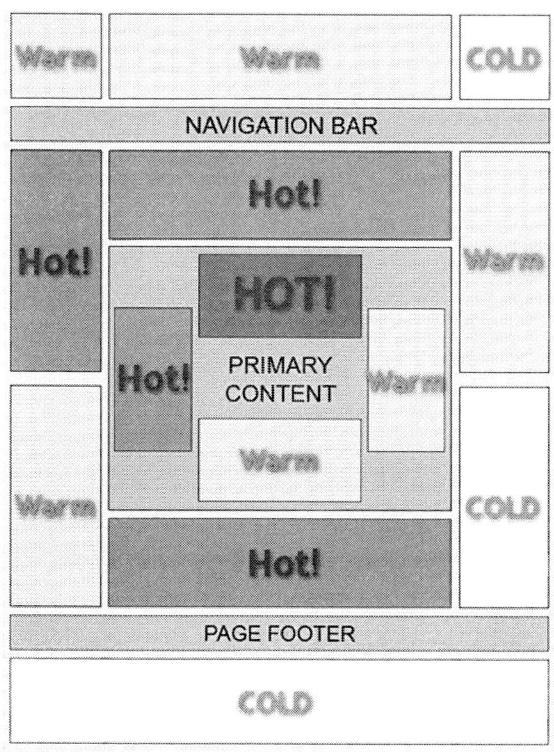

How does it work? When you look at a website, Google has determined (using eye studies) that there are certain places that people automatically look, (the hot spots) and there are certain places that they skip over, as those are usually where ads are placed. Those are the cold spots. When you want someone to do something on your website, like sign up for your e-newsletter, read your latest blog post, or buy your products or services, put your conversion form, most compelling pictures, and incentives into the "hot spots" of the heat map.

Using this map as a model will help you put your information where people will be most likely to read it, and will help you increase people buying on your website.

Here's where you'll notice what a lot of nonprofit websites do incorrectly, and a lot of business websites too. They'll have their donate button or buy button at the far right of the navigation bar, or they'll have it on the bottom right hand or top right of the page. This is the WORST place to put your call to action. Whatever your call to action is, then do yourself a favor and put it where you can make sure people will click on it.

If you'd like to get a LOT more scientific and efficient with your website design, research User Experience design (UX) or User Interface Design (UI). Check out some recorded webinars on http://eBoostConsulting.com***. You can also try using http://VisualWebsiteOptimizer.com or http://Optomizely.com to do A/B testing different aspects of your design. A/B testing is taking different parts of your website and changing them for new visitors over a given period of time, to see which changes get you more sales****.

What we just talked about is called Conversion Rate Optimization, aka CRO. This means you have a plan for the person that comes to your website, you figure out what their major objections are, and then you focus on getting them to give you their email address or buy. Want more conversion tips to get people to buy? Here's a list of 544 tips*****.

What about "Focus Above the Fold?"

With the advent of many different screen sizes on iPads, tablets, iPhones and other mobile devices, focusing above the fold on your website (before people have to scroll down to see more) is becoming a bit dated.

Must Know

You have to think about every kind of question a person can have on levels 1-2 of the ladder, and write to that person. This is where the majority of people are, this is how they will first find you if they're doing a Google search, and this is where you can start to establish your credibility with them.

Must Do

If you haven't already done so, set up your domain, hosting, and Wordpress blog.

1. Buy your Domain. Go to http://Joker.com and see if the domain you want is available.
2. Don't go for the cheapest hosting, because it will make your website load slowly, and people will not wait around, and you'll lose sales. The cheapest hosting will also go down much more frequently. People can't buy from you if your website is down. Try Dreamhost or http://AriesLabs.com.
3. Go to http://FreeWPThemes.net if you'd like a free Wordpress theme. Don't try any other free Wordpress theme websites

***For example, http://www.eboostconsulting.com/conversion-design-maximizing-site-roi

****http://www.smashingmagazine.com/2010/06/24/the-ultimate-guide-to-a-b-testing/

*****http://unbounce.com/conversion-rate-optimization/544-conversion-rate-optimization-tips/

though, because they can have harmful malware embedded in them. If you want to spend a little money, I recommend the Headway or SimplePress themes.

4. Activate some useful plugins for your new blog. Here is a list of Best Wordpress Plugins that will drive conversions. There is a bigger list in the workbook.
    - Cool Ryan Easy Pop-ups: Pop-Up Opt-in
    - Headspace 2
    - p3 Profiler
    - Wordpress Mobile Pack
    - Yoast Breadcrumbs
    - Network Publisher

What did you learn?

- What is the ladder of engagement?
- How can you create a section on your site that speaks to levels 2-3 of this ladder?
- What kind of web hosting should you buy?
- What's a good platform for your website?

More books to learn about this:

Convert! By Ben Hunt
Cashvertising by Drew Eric Whitman

Chapter 6.2: The gold is in your list, AKA e-newsletters

What is it? An e-newsletter is an email newsletter that you might send once a week or once a month to keep your name at the forefront of people's minds.	**When to do it** Sign up with a newsletter service right now. The sooner you start building your list, the sooner you are going to have a bunch of people wanting to buy your stuff.
What you'll need An e-newsletter software account. A pdf as a prize, or an auto-responder or something else. A good idea of where you want your signup box to go on your website.	**What to do:** Once you've signed up, put together 5 newsletters and wait until you've got 5-10 signups before scheduling them to go out.

This chapter will cover:

- What makes a good Opt-in form
- How to get MORE people to sign up for your emails
- Subject Lines to get people to open
- 16 kinds of headlines to help your customers buy
- The 5 reasons people share your e-newsletter
- How to format your e-newsletter
- Sample survey questions to help you segment your subscribers
- Lots of ways to build your email list
- When to send your emails, and more!

Where do your customers start their day? With Email! Want proof? Look at the diagram on the next page.

Think about where you start YOUR day. Even if people are not on Twitter or Facebook, they will have email, and many people check their email as soon as they wake up. You can be there, in their inbox, reminding them of all the value you bring.

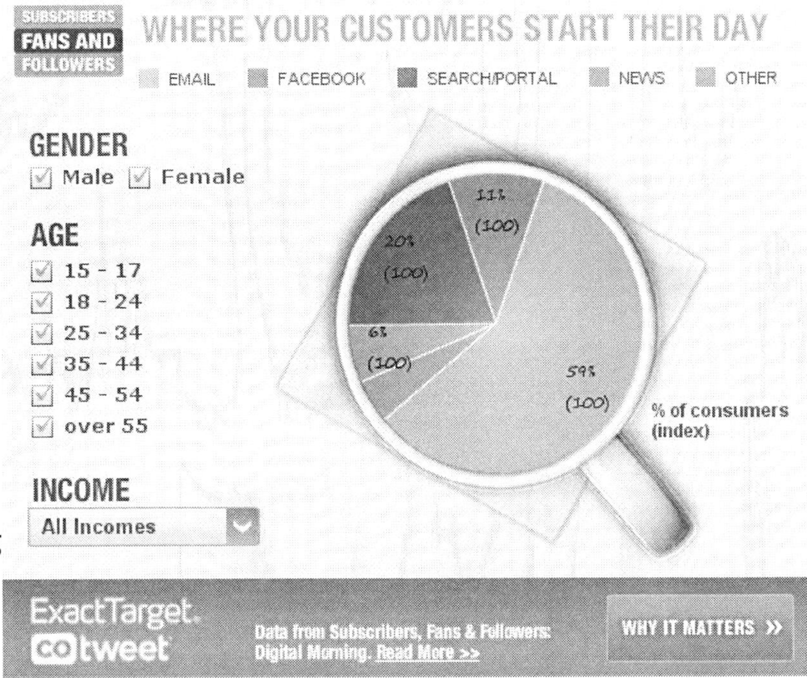

Email is the most powerful social media tool you have. When you have a large list that you've communicated with consistently, you can get your list to support your business or nonprofit.

The single most important factor that will hold you back in business is lack of customers. Your consistent e-newsletter is a way to communicate your value and give free things to your list, so that they will tell their friends about you, and you will get more and more people signing up to your list every week. But mailing every week isn't enough. You have to be constantly looking for new ways to grow your list.

John Jantsch, the author of a book on social media called; *The Referral Engine* says, "*Businesses should not use social media until they have email nailed"* and frankly, I agree.

How many email messages get opened across industries?

It depends on the industry you're in, but if you get above a 10% open rate, according to Mailchimp*, you are doing remarkably well.

What is the best format for your emails?

---

*http://www.mailchimp.com/resources/research/email-marketing-benchmarks-by-industry

According to Dr. Drew Whitman, the best format is HTML. 60% of people can open HTML emails. The bad news is, you don't know which 60% you're mailing to. And it used to be that you would have to choose. But you don't have to. You can have a plain text version as well as an HTML version. You don't even have to make it complex and full of fancy templates. I prefer to keep mine simple, with just a logo at the top.

Who should you use to manage your email list?

There are lots of options. Aweber.com, MadMimi.com and MailChimp.com, just to name a few. Research who some of your e-newsletter heroes are using, and go take a free trial to see if you like them.

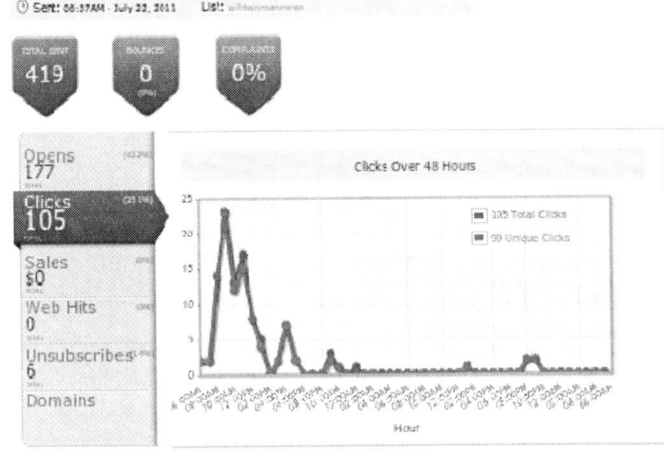

You should choose an e-newsletter software that helps you make tons of conversion forms easily. In this context, a conversion form is simply an e-newsletter signup form that allows you to give the subscriber something in exchange for their email address.

A good e-newsletter software allows you to check and see how many people opened your email, and mail directly to the people who emailed and the people who clicked. The screenshot from Aweber (*above*) shows the number of people opening the email, when they opened it, and a big button so you can send JUST to those people.

How often should you send your e-newsletter?

According to Forrester Research and Dr. Drew Whitman, the majority of people prefer to have an email once a week if they sign up for an e-newsletter. ** If that sounds daunting to you, start with once a month and build up to it. Just remember, the more time you sink into building community and communicating consistently, the more it will pay off. Imagine you're building a friendship with your readers. How often do you communicate with your closest friends? Once a week? If so, make sure you treat your current and potential customers the same way. Sending between 8am and 9am in the morning is best, because it is also the time that people generally open their emails.

How should you design your e-newsletter?

For online reading, sans serif fonts are the best. Serif fonts are fonts with extra curly things on them, like Times New Roman. Sans Serif, fonts like Arial and Verdana are consistently voted the most readable fonts. What size? 12 point is the best.***

You should also know that putting short tiny paragraphs together is more effective than huge walls of text.

So writing an
e-newsletter
with this kind
of formatting
will help you
get read more.

Other formatting tips:

- Make sure you have a text only version that can stand alone, without pictures.
- Test it on a smart phone, in Yahoo, in Gmail, in Outlook.
- The Google Heatmap also applies to e-newsletters. Make sure it looks like your website and has the most important content in the hot spots.

How to write compelling, shareable e-newsletters?

Why do we share e-newsletter?

1. To bring valuable and entertaining content to others
2. To define ourselves to others

** 30-35% of people said they'd like to receive emails once a week, 18% said two or three days per week, 13% said once a month, 12% said daily, 10% said two or three times per month, 6% said less than once per month, and 8% said never. *Cashvertising,* Drew Eric Whitman. pg. 166.

***Ibid. *Cashvertising* by Drew Eric Whitman.

3. To grow and nourish our relationships
4. Self-fulfillment

First, you start with the subject line. People who don't even open your e-newsletter are not going to be able to buy your stuff or donate to you. Your subject lines have to be KILLER because they have to compete with everything else in this person's inbox. You have to answer: What's In It For Me? (WIIFM)

Here are some compelling subject lines, according to Dr. Drew Eric Whitman, author of Cashvertising:

1. Free
2. New
3. At last
4. This
5. Announcing
6. Warning!
7. Just released
8. Now
9. Here's
10. These

These are just 10 samples. If you want more, check out Mr. Whitman's book. The Neuroscience Marketing blog is also good. (http://neurosciencemarketing.com/blog)

How do I know these subject lines work? Because I've used them myself. Check out some of the subject lines I've used by browsing through my e-newsletter archives at http://wildwomanfundraising.com/free-stuff. I got my open rate to jump from 10% to 40% almost overnight. And since I have taught webinars on this subject, I've heard from my students that their open rates have nearly doubled with new subject lines.

Top Tip! To make your subject line POP, use the word YOU.

Once they've opened the email, what will have people falling over themselves to buy your products? You have to study the greats, AND find your own voice. Sign up for other people's email lists and see what they do. You can also sign up for my list at http://wildsocialmedia.com. Dr. Mercola at http://mercola.com, is a master of email marketing. I'd highly recommend signing up for his email list just to see how he makes compelling copy. You don't have to agree with him about anything. Just read his subject lines and his headlines.

Another way to learn how to write a compelling e-newsletter is to read *Cashvertising* by Drew Eric Whitman, who has some good words that will help people open your e-newsletter[****]. There are also certain words that will get your e-newsletter marked as spam. I've listed a few of them in this post[*****]. And finally, practice makes perfect! Sending out your own e-newsletter every week will help you get better in no time.

Here are 16 Types of headlines you can create:

- Story
- News
- Reasons Why
- Item - Hype
- Finality
- List
- Curiosity
- Expert Positioning
- Extreme Value Proposition
- Testimonial
- Warning
- Dominant Emotion
- If...Then
- Straight Benefit
- Offer
- Question

What should you write about?

Your activities: If you're giving a presentation or doing an event, definitely talk about that.

Useful free advice: If you've written a blog post or two since you sent out the last e-newsletter, link them.

Help other people in your industry: If you're doing a link round-up of interesting articles in your industry, make sure to put that in as well.

Joking around: I like to add a little bit of fun into my e-newsletter, everything from here's what we did over the weekend to here's a

****http://www.wildsocialmedia.com/how-to-email-e-newsletter/

*****http://www.wildsocialmedia.com/are-you-writing-an-e-newsletter-whatever-you-do-dont-use-these-words/

drawing with some useful tips for you!

If you're really not sure what to write about, look at some of the keywords that lead people to your website, or what people are copy-pasting from your site, because they find it useful. Use Tynt.com to figure this out. I've written more about this here: http://www.wildsocialmedia.com/people-copy-paste-website.

Evaluate your current newsletter. Are you bringing valuable or entertaining content? Ask yourself, would I share this? Look at the Smithsonian Institution e-newsletter as an example of consistent, compelling content. They have billions of dollars and they are using some of the best people in the world to write their e-newsletters for them.

Remember, your subscribers are learning. You're giving them new information. Are you taking them on a journey?

If you're struggling to build your email list, this next part will help you.

Here's the first step. Make different e-newsletter signup forms, aka conversion beacons for different kinds of people who come to your website.

A conversion is the visitor taking the right action on your website. So what do you want people to do once they get to your website?

Sample conversions:

1. Give you their email address.
2. Buy your ebook
3. Donate to your nonprofit
4. Take your survey
5. Follow you on Twitter
6. Subscribe to your RSS feed
7. Send you an email requesting a consultation

If you have two or three things that you want people to do, then you'll want to segment people who want different things. For example, I have a signup form that teaches people 50 secrets of fundraising, another one about sponsorships, another one about fundraising jobs, and another one that just pops up when people open the website for the first time. I also have one that I put at the bottom of my blog posts sometimes.

What services should you use for e-newsletter conversion form design?

If you use Constant Contact, they only allow you to use 1 conversion form. Other e-newsletter software vendors, like Aweber, allow you to make as many as you want. I prefer Aweber for this reason. You can try Mailchimp, MadMimi, iContact, and others.

How to Make an E-newsletter Sign-up form, aka a Conversion Beacon

How do you convert visits to sales? One way to do it is to start with a Conversion Beacon. In this case, we'll discuss user forms, and specifically, e-newsletter opt-in forms.

A Conversion Beacon is when you ask people to do something. One of the most popular ways to convert people is to use a conversion form.

You can see an example of a conversion form from Yaro Starak at http://Entrepreneurs-Journey.com on the next page.

This conversion form worked on me! It shows me what I get, it SCREAMS benefits not features, it's got arrows and the button is circled. Nice!

A conversion form in this case means you are gathering people's names to put on your email list, so that when the time comes for you to ask for their testimonials, or to invite them to be your clients, you've got people who have opted in to getting more communications from you, you get them thinking about you more often, if you send out emails every week or every month, and make them that much more likely to buy things from you.

Here's a screenshot of one of my conversion forms.

What fields should you have in your conversion form?

You can see I've got a place for the name, and for email. If you make this too complicated, like, First, Last, How you heard, etc, people don't want to fill it in.

What pictures should you have on your conversion form?

Make the button say the thing they want. Not just "Sign up" but WHY they want to sign up! For example: "Give me my free ebook" could be on the button, or "Get Instant Access" or "Yes! I want more money!" You get the picture. Put in the benefit to the customer. A picture of what you're giving them at the top doesn't hurt either. Notice how I have a picture of money. Yaro Starak uses a picture of his ebook and a picture of a pdf symbol. You might give people a free song, if you're a musician, or something else.

What else should you have on your conversion form?
You need to make it look as easy as possible to sign up. Simple and clean. What makes a form look simple and clean? According to *Web Design for ROI: Turning Browsers into Buyers & Prospects into Leads* by Lance Loveday and Sandra Niehaus, you need:

White space. *Leave enough empty space—whatever the color—around the form and between the form rows. This improves legibility and scannability.*

Removal of all extraneous elements. *Everything in, on, and around a form should contribute to its completion and submission.*

Clear label-field association. *There is such a thing as too much space, especially when it's between a field and its label. Too much space here makes visitors try to track horizontally across a blank area hoping to end up at the correct field. Strongly associate the field with the label by positioning them closely together.*

Legible text. *Make sure the form text doesn't send visitors diving text for their reading glasses. Tiny, low-contrast text (like pale gray on a white background) is difficult to read on a computer monitor. The text used for form field labels and inside the fields themselves should be high-contrast, uncomplicated typography that's easy to read.* ******

(this means black text on a white background, with a sans serif font, like Arial, is best.)

Why should people opt-in? Give a pay-off

Make it exciting to sign up for your newsletter by offering a free resource when they sign up. You can have a 3 email auto-responder to teach people how to do something. Or offer a free 30 page pdf or white paper of how to do something that speaks directly to the pains of your potential client or customer. When I asked people why they signed up for my e-newsletter, a few people told me they signed up just because they liked my writing. So sometimes people will go for the free prize, and other times they just like you and want to read more of your writing.

Think about what you want to offer as a payoff to opt-in to your newsletter.

Think about what problems people have. Do you want to offer a free ten page e-book on one of their problems?

(For example, a lot of people are out of work right now. I've got an ebook attached to my sign-up that lets people have 30 pages of free step-by-step advice on how to get their next nonprofit job.) Or, perhaps "Finding your audience as a post-classical composer," or "How to be psychic" or "How to figure out your life path."

******Loveday, Lance. Niehaus, Sandra. *Web Design for ROI: Turning Browsers into Buyers & Prospects into Leads.* Pearson, 2008

Make a little picture of what you are offering people, and put in a photograph of what your ebook represents.

Format your opt-in form

Make sure that the color scheme matches your website. When deciding how wide or tall it should be, find out the exact pixel width of your side-bar? You can find out how wide your sidebar is by installing the Firefox Firebug plugin.

Where should the opt-in form go?

Ideally, you want it at the top so that people will see it first. You also want it within the Google heat map F shape, so the center or top left is ideal. You can also make your opt-in form pop up in the center.

Make a different format for your in-line opt-in form

When someone has just finished reading your article, or even half-way through, you can give them the option to sign up again. This way, if they just learned something new, or were entertained by your writing, they will have a chance to show you they want more information from you, by signing up right there.

How to get more e-newsletter signups right now

Idea #1: Partner & Provide Value:

Doing a guest webinar, guest blog post, or guest teleconference call with clients or a partner.

Idea #2: Going to networking events:

After you get someone's card, ask people if they'd like to be on your email list. (Note: Don't just automatically add them if you've got their business card. This has happened to me, and I think it's kinda rude, and not implied consent if you've got someone's card to add them to your list.)

Idea #3: Grab them when they first get there with a hover form.

Design your hover opt-in form. This one should say, “Hey, are you new here? Try out my newsletter, where I'll give you monthly, weekly or daily tips about “BMW motorcycles” or “dog breeding” or anything else you are an expert in.

Idea #4: Put your e-newsletter signup at the bottom of the page as well as top left.

Let's say that someone has just finished reading one of your incredible articles. Why not grab them while they're digesting it, and say, hey, sign up for my e-newsletter? That can happen at the end of the post or at the bottom of each page on your website.

Idea #5: Give a free webinar or conference call

Another way to get more email signups is to give a free webinar or conference call on an important and useful topic. What webinar service should you use? I've used Instant Presenter and Readytalk, but found GotoWebinar to be the most reliable. Do your own research on this though. Once you've gotten the word out about your webinar, people will start signing up for it. And you can download those names as a .csv file, and add them to your e-newsletter list, legally.

Idea #6: Run a contest

A contest, such as a tagline contest, or marketing contest to test how well your readers are marketing what they do, is a wonderful way to get people to sign up for your e-newsletter, AND position yourself as an authority in this area. Pepsi is famous for their “Pepsi Challenge” contest and that was a HUGE email list building technique for them. Is there a contest that you could run? Maybe a giveaway for your readers or followers on Twitter? Think about a contest that YOU would sign up for.

Idea #7: Link other industry bloggers & tell them you did it.

A friend of mine does this and it works to help her develop goodwill with different people in her industry. And they link her more, and talk with her more, and she gets more e-newsletter signups. It's marvelous, a circle of goodwill that just keeps rippling outwards. I make a point to link her in my e-newsletters, and I've started to do this as well. Before you make people want to be friends with you, you have to be friendly with them.

Idea #8: Be consistent with your e-newsletters.

This will help more people know about you, and sign up for your e-newsletter, especially if you put a link at the bottom for them to forward the email to a friend. Believe me. You will get far more subscribers than unsubscribes. I like to do once a week because this is what my heroes do, but you could try once a month to start.

Idea #9: Do a giveaway with other bloggers

I did this recently and got 300 new subscribers. How it works: You agree to have an industry goodies giveaway. You all promote it on your e-newsletters, Twitter, and other channels. Then the link takes everyone to one page that has a bunch of goodies on it, everything from a free chapter of your book to a white paper or e-article that is particularly useful, or a whole ebook plus consultation time. Each person in the giveaway is listed separately, so each visitor to the site can come and get different things that they need. This leads to lots of new people finding out about you and how helpful you can be.

Idea #10: Write a whitepaper

What is a whitepaper? It's a short paper, often no more than 12 pages long, that talks about a challenge and opportunity in your sector, and offers research on solutions to that issue. This research can be culled from journal articles, qualitative interviews or quantitative surveys of people in your industry.

Why write a whitepaper? It establishes more credibility than a blog post. AND You can give it away in exchange for someone signing up for your email list. How do you write a whitepaper? Michael Stelzner, who wrote the book on Whitepapers, has lots of tips for you on his website. He also wrote a book called Launch! Which talks about more ways to build your email list.

Idea #11: Do original research on a problem in your industry and write a report on it.

Then you can give this report away as a gift for signing up for your enewsletter. This is similar to a whitepaper but it can be longer. For example, NTEN.org surveys their members and comes out with a research report on the best donor databases for different kinds of nonprofits, and what the pros and cons of each database are. It's comprehensive and probably gives them lots of enewsletter signups.

After they fill out your form, how can you gather more information about your subscribers?

Put a survey in your welcome email. Ask questions such as:

- Why did you sign up?
- Where did you hear about us?
- What are you looking for?
- What are some of your goals right now?
- What do you need?

What about after they put in their name and email? You can redirect to another page with more demographic information they can fill out.

You can emphasize that they only need to put in their name and email, but ask for their address, phone, and a problem they're having right now that you can help solve.

You can also do a survey of your subscribers and offer a prize for them to complete the survey.

When they complete your survey, you can segment your target audience. Are you looking for:

- New customers or donors
- To retain customers or donors
- To upgrade current loyal customers
- To introduce yourself in a new area
- Speaking opportunities or something else?

When you segment your list you can give the exact right offer to each person.

If they won't take the survey, you can at least segment your list by people who often open your emails and people who rarely open your emails.

Must Know

- Be consistent. Send out an e-newsletter every week.
- 12 point Arial font for your e-newsletter
- Have an HTML and a plain text version.
- You'll get more sign-ups if you give people lots of reasons to sign up for your e-newsletter.

Must Do

- Give away subscriber-only rewards.
- Survey your subscribers and segment your list.
- Put your conversion beacon in the hot spots of the heat map.
- Try an auto-responder to help people feel connected over time.

End of Chapter Questions:

What is a conversion beacon?
What fields should you have in your e-newsletter signup?
What can you promise to increase conversions?
What should you put in your opt-in form?
What are the different kinds of opt-in forms?

Chapter 6.3: Your Blogging Roadmap

What is it? Blogging is the way to get found, have people look at you as an authority, and have people buy from you. It's also a good way to become a better writer.	**When to do it:** Blog at least once a month. In the beginning, blogging 5 days a week will get you lots more traffic, and make you a better writer. Keep yourself on a blogging schedule.
What you'll need: Joker.com (domain registration & lookup) Domain name Hosting Wordpress theme Newsletter conversion form Wordpress plugins Graphic designer Web developer	**What to do:** Go to Joker.com and find a domain name based around your name or niche. Buy the domain for 2 years, then look at hosting. The cheapest hosting is not good. I like Dreamhost or Arieslabs.com. Find a Wordpress theme or find a blog that you like and get a graphic designer to create your version of it. Get a web developer to put this theme up on your domain. *Fill out the blogging worksheets in the back of the book.*

REMEMBER:

"You need to build Content, Context, Connection, and Community" -John Jantsch, *The Referral Engine*

England

I started blogging back in 1999. I had a Diaryland diary. I was living in England and wanted people back home to have a way of checking up on me, without having to write the same email ten times.

I remember sitting in the computer center, late at night, staring at the screen until my eyes blurred. I remember the giant monitors, and trying to read my required reading online instead of having to buy a book. I remember listening to Dutch radio online. I remember the smell of the industrial carpet worn down by years of muddy student feet. I remember the loneliness but strange beauty stumbling out into the pre-dawn light with some odd piece of writing posted back to my family thousands of miles away. Blog posts about the funny differences between England and America, about a dream I had, or maybe about a movie I had watched with my film buff friend Ealasaid. Around that time I remember thinking how much I wanted my own website, but I didn't know anyone who could help me make one.

Fast forward to 2005. I finally had a friend who could help me make a website. It was sketchy and pitiful, but it was up. I put my art up there and actually made a couple of sales.

Want to publish a book? Can you blog that?

Fast forward again. In August of 2009 I went to the Willamette Writer's Conference where I talked to different agents representing different publishers. They all said the same thing. "Do you have a platform? If not, no publisher will even look at you!" A platform meant "a readership" which meant **"If you are not online or not already famous you have no credibility with any publisher."**

So in November 2009, thanks to the help of Steve Havelka, I started my blog, Wild Woman Fundraising.com, named after my book, The Wild Woman's Guide to Fundraising. I never knew how much I could write, (despite graduating with a degree in writing) until I decided to write five blog posts a week for a year. And I did it. When I published my book in November 2010, I immediately had sales all over the world, from England to Canada to Tasmania, from Finland to New York City.

At the time of this writing, (October 2012) I blog 1-3 days per week, and my traffic is higher than ever. I have made thousands of dollars from this website in sales, in consulting services, in speaking engagements, and more. People subscribe to my newsletter, ask me questions, engage in my Twitter chats, and I have nearly 21,000 monthly readers. It's taken me almost 24 months to get this far, but wow. I never thought I could have such a popular website!

Want to help others?

After the success I'd had with my book, I decided that I wanted to help other people have the same success that I did. It was obvious that my site was a reputation engine, helping me build my reputation around the web. My writing helps the people looking for my keywords get advice and hire me, attend my webinars and buy my products. So I started my company, Wild Social Media, to help people get more customers and more cash.

As you can see from the story above, blogging is now a way to have a business, not just a way to journal in public.

Don't get me wrong, blogging does not replace having a business or marketing plan, or sales, or product creation or networking in person. It's simply a piece of your marketing strategy that you can't afford to ignore. When people see you as a resource, they'll come back to see what else you have to say.

Blogging is also known as Content marketing

The problem is: People don't know who you are, or what you know. They don't care about you. Until you start blogging, providing value to them, then they start to care about you, and your tribe finds you.

Blogging/Content Marketing has so many benefits, it's hard to count them all.

Benefits of Blogging

What are some benefits of blogging? According to Shel Israel and Robert Scoble, when you blog, you become:

1. **Publishable.** You can become a publisher in an afternoon. You don't have to wait for permission or go through barriers to get your ideas out there.
2. **Findable.** People start to know you as an authority in your field, because you're so prolific. You become more findable.

3. **Social.** Your site looks ACTIVE and looks like you're engaging in conversation with your visitors/potential customers.
4. **Viral.** Your post can spread quicker than a news service.
5. **Syndicatable.** RSS means people can get your post within seconds of the time you publish it. No newspaper or magazine in the world can be that fast.
6. **Linkable.** Through your blog, you can link to millions of other places on the internet. People have a place to find you, and a place to go find other things, when they come to your blog.*

More Benefits of Blogging
I would add, when you blog,

You become a RESOURCE. People have a reason to come back to your site again and again.

Improved communication skills. Writing under pressure, over and over again makes you a better writer, and by proxy, a better communicator.

Money! You can re-purpose your posts into products, such as e-books, physical books, podcasts, interviews, videos, and more.

Why aren't we talking about SEO?

SEO stands for Search Engine Optimization. You can certainly do everything you can to create a website full of keywords that you want Google to rank you for.

Unfortunately whatever I tell you about SEO in this book will be obsolete in a few weeks. But you will be FINDABLE anyway if your posts are legitimately popular. Remember. Google will rank your website if a lot of people visit it, and if a lot of trustworthy sites (like .edu and .gov) link to you. The only way to get those links is to be genuinely helpful. So content marketing, aka blogging, is what truly works over time.

Top tip! Fresh, useful, engaging content with lots of readers trumps SEO tricks every time.

Are you alive? Blogging tells us.

---

*Scoble, Robert. Israel, Shel. *Naked Conversations.*

Recently I was teaching a social media workshop to small business owners, and I asked, "*Who here checks out a website's blog first, to see how active it is, before deciding to contact the business*?" And lots of people raised their hands. Then I asked, "*And if there hasn't been any activity for a year or two, do you assume they are no longer in business*?" "Yes," people said.

Like it or not, we have to keep producing content to show we are in business, because we are all media companies now.

Let's face it, you would not want to keep up a business blog unless there was a concrete business reason to do so. It's not just about making sales, it's about showing that you're still alive. It's also about helping people know, like and trust you, moving them from accident to ally, in the shortest amount of time possible.

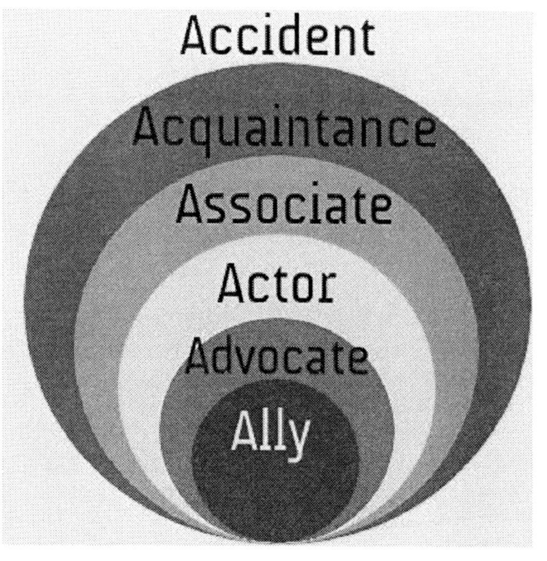

Marketing Concepts:
How do you build relationships online? The same way you do offline. Provide free, useful things to people. And you'll become a resource. And then they'll think of you if they have a question. And then they'll refer their friends to you if THEY have questions.

According to Anne Baber and Lynne Waymon, you have to touch people a lot of times before they become allies for your business.

On the internet, and in networking meetings, People find you by *Accident.*
You need to touch them 5 more times before they are an *Acquaintance.*
You must touch them another 5 times before they are an *Associate.*
Touch them 5 MORE times before they are an *Actor,*
Touch them another 5 times before they are an *Advocate,*
And finally, touch them another 5 times before they are an *Ally.***

**This concept comes from Lynne Waymon and Anne Baber's book, *Making Your Contacts Count.* I have created the diagram above to illustrate their point.

An ally will consistently refer people to you again and again. You want as many allies as possible. This only happens after you've built trust. When people first meet you, they have no reason to trust you. If you continue to consistently write useful, free content, people will move through being an advocate and ally for you.

But instead of just one person at a time, a blog and e-newsletter and social media presence allows you to build relationships with people all over the world, all at once.

But providing useful, meaningful, free content is hard. How can you keep up your pace, day after day, week after week?

Writing Your Blog Posts

You can be a Researcher, A Reporter and a Role Model.

- *A Researcher* reads the latest books, articles, and blog posts for the industry and informs people about useful pieces of information in blog posts. This is also known as content curation.

- *A Reporter* interviews top minds in the field, building relationships, including book reviews and author interviews. I love this method. This is how Oprah started.

- *A Role Model* is someone who is at the top of their field, who answers questions and describes what solutions they would do for given problems, and encourages others to succeed.

Each of these methods lends itself well to blog posts and other ways to get your content onto the internet.

"I have to penetrate this chattering and this meaningless debate that is occupying most of my attention. I have to come up with some one thing that really speaks to my deepest interest. Otherwise I nod off in one way or another. So to find that urgent...(thing) takes a lot of version and a lot of work and a lot of sweat."

-Leonard Cohen[***]

If you're worried about blogging, if you think that nobody cares what you have to say, or that you can't write, or that you don't know what you would ever write about, remember the quote above from Leonard

*** Leonard Cohen, interviewed in *Songwriters on Songwriting*, by Paul Zollo

Cohen. You have to find something that speaks to your deepest interest.

For me, when I built my first business blog, it was writing about the injustices of the nonprofit world, and how to make the work world a better place. That kept me going for YEARS. And as I built my business, my new passion became helping other small business owners learn how to market themselves online.

"The easier it is for people to understand, the better it is, I think. If you can capture something that you feel is real and express it in a way that a lot of people can understand, that's rare and there's something about that that makes a piece have a certain kind of life.

-Paul Simon****

This quote on songwriting is also applicable to blogging. You must make your posts easy to understand. You can capture something that you feel, express it, have it help others in a similar situation, and then, if you've built your blog correctly, your content marketing will start to take off. People will come to read your blog or open your e-newsletters just for your writing alone. And from there, they will tell their friends, forward your articles, and you will get more traffic and customers.

What to Write About First?

Use this diagram.

Your Customer's Problem	Your Customer's Goal	Your Customer's Agenda	Your Customer's Pain	Your Solution

Now instead of using it for keywords, use it for your first blog posts. Think about: What problems to your potential customers have? What is their goal? What's their agenda? What are they trying to accomplish? What's their pain? How can you take away their pain? How can you solve their problem? What's your solution?

Top tips for blogging:

Provide Value consistently

- Blog one to five days per week.

**** Ibid.

- Ask people to weigh in with their ideas. Ask your readers what they want to know.
- Engage with your readers in your comments, provide even more advice.

Be Provocative

- Entertain, perplex, and inform.
- Use examples from the news, from history, from novels, from conventional wisdom or myths.
- Your own real-life stories can be powerful.

People will share your content if:

- It is polarizing, controversial.
- It states a basic fundamental truth that's worth repeating.
- It shows a step by step process to success in your niche that comes from your years of experience or research.

I know this sounds like a lot of work. It is. But you can mix and match your blogging strategies. You don't have to blog 5 days a week. Even just blogging once a month is somewhere to begin.

If you need a place to start, remember the ladder of engagement from Chapter 6, and make a series of posts for level 1-2 of the ladder.

If you've already got several blog posts, and you want to see what content is most popular on your site, then use Tynt. The most common way that people share information from your website is by cutting and pasting text off of it into a text document or an email. Tynt.com will show you what people find valuable on your site. It will show you what keywords bring people to your site, it will show you what people copied from your site, and it will show how they shared your content. If you notice a trend in what people are copying, make a series of blog posts around this subject. Signing up with Tynt is simple and free and they'll give you an emailed report every week on what people copy from your site. Go to http://tynt.com to get started.

If you've already got resources you can put online, like presentations, whitepapers, or pdfs, put them up at http://scribd.com. You can see which articles are the most popular, and create products or content on your blog based around what your potential customers want.

If you're a big company, get everyone together to make a

blog.

When you're deciding to create a blog for your company, get a variety of departments together, such as Marketing, PR, Search Optimization, Customer Service, IT and Social Media.

Why should you do that?

Because you need to learn the language of your customers' pain. You even need to know the minutiae of their pain.

This way, when Marketing wants to put together a package, Customer Service will be able to tell them the features customers crave. When Search Optimization wants to put together a blog with keywords, PR will have been listening and be able to add their ideas to the site. When IT and social media teams get together with all the rest, the IT team will be able to tell people what is possible, and the social media team will be able to carry everyone's vision into the different social media channels.

What if you're a small company? What do you blog about?

How can you be contrarian and wild and create content all at once?

- **Look at your competitors: Praise them**. Imagine how contrary that is! You're supposed to be attacking them, but you praise them instead! Wow!

- **Imagine you can say the forbidden things**. What would you admit? What would you finally say, that you've wanted to say for years? Write that post. You are going to gain so much social trust based on your blatant honesty.

- **Go to an event**: Joke about how it was run. Offer to help them improve it.

- **Get inspired by your passions**, relate them to your business: Make an extremely crazy analogy. Reach for it. Try to make these two things relate.

- **Q&A with your customers**: Tell them that they're wrong. Go on. Sometimes the customer ISN'T always right.

- **Tell HOW to do something**: Use your experience in your field and tell people what they've been taught is wrong.
- **Interview Luminaries**: And disagree with them.
- **Share photos**: Of your mom. Sometimes people want to see that you're human, you know?
- **Go behind the scenes**: Be open about ideas that don't work out. Show your napkin sketches.
- **Share productivity tips**: Show off, and help people.
- **Host an event**: Either virtual or in person. If no one shows up, make up some funny characters that came. Talk about their weird lives.
- **Find content and post it**: Curating content is fun. For awhile. Don't rely on this though. People want to see your original thoughts as well. Unless you're going to mix it up by curating the stupidest things you've found written about your field, and the truest things, and then how people have turned a sacred belief from your niche inside out.
- **Look at the news for your industry or look at current events.** Talk about how it relates to what you're doing. Or talk about how it has no effect on what you're doing at all.
- **Go to your archives**: Go spelunking. Are there any hidden places in there that you could explore a little more? What were some popular posts? Why not recap or revise them?
- **Get guest posts**: By people who are contrary too!
- **Showcase your viewer's ideas and comments.** Especially the inflammatory ones. When people disagree, let them disagree. If people are going to be compelled to get involved on your site, make it hard for them to NOT leave a comment.
- **Monitor your keywords**: If someone ignorant or sold out is talking about your field, get on that, comment on their blog, and then turn that comment into a post. Tell them how you feel.

Check out this graphic from Marketing Sherpa on the next page.

As you can see, content creation was rated the most effective way to get more traffic. That includes blogging, but it's not limited to that. It can also be enewsletters, youtube videos, and more.

Remember, blogging is not easy, but it pays off over time in ways you can't even imagine right now.

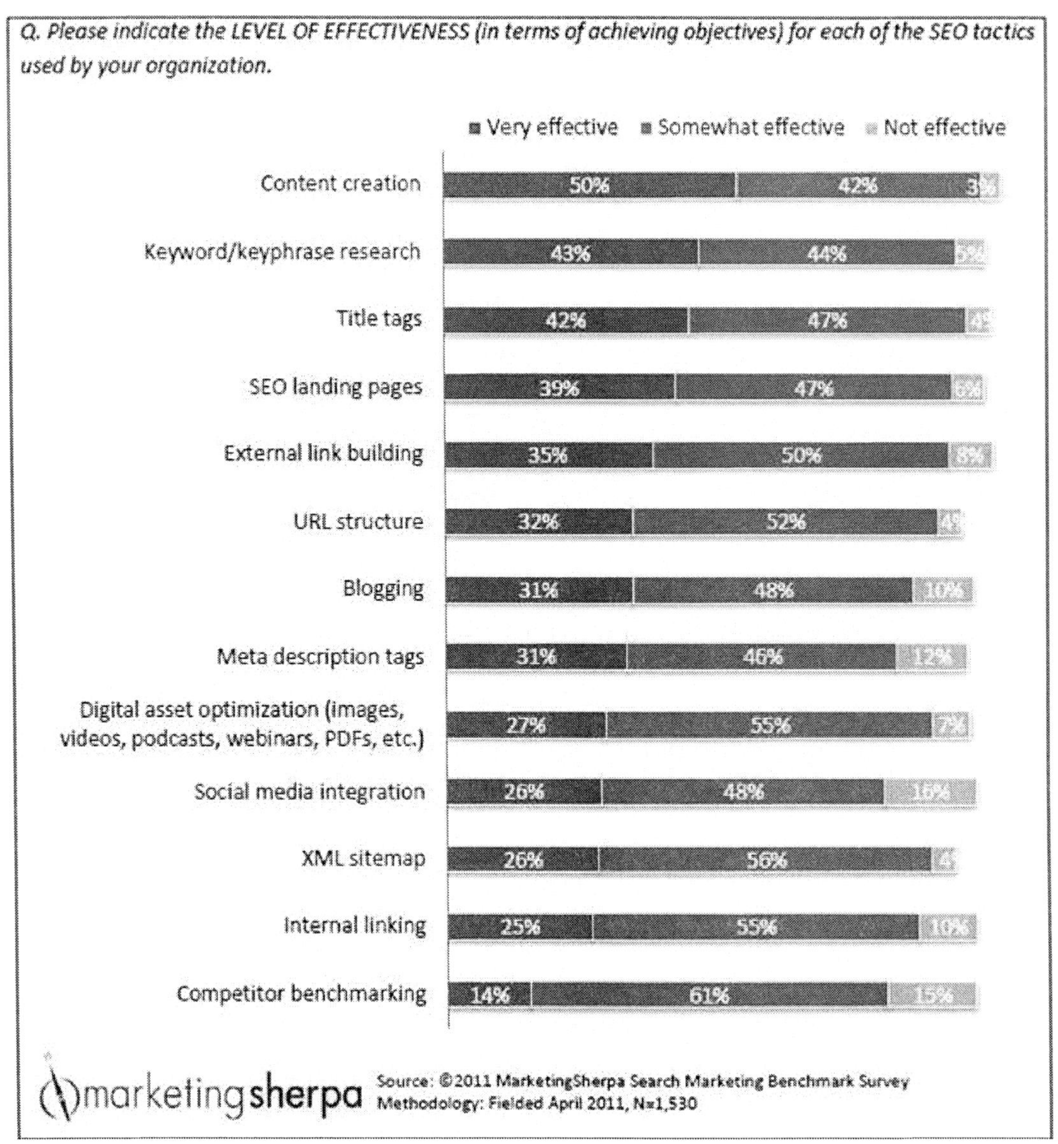

Reader Questions:

What are the six pillars of blogging, according to Scoble and Israel?
What are five sources of blog post ideas?
What can a blog do for you?

Must Know

- Blogging 5 days a week for a year is a good way to get traffic & community.
- Cheap hosting will hurt you more than it helps you.

Must Do

- Create content that speaks to level 1 and 2 of the ladder of engagement.
- Create posts that speak to people's pain, agenda, costs, and goals.

More Blogging Resources:

My Blogging Webinar Series on http://WildSocialMedia.com
Naked Conversations book by Shel Israel & Robert Scoble
Content Rules book by Anne Handey & C.C. Chapman
The Referral Engine by John Jantsch

Chapter 6.4: LinkedIn = Fabulous for your Reputation

What is it? LinkedIn is a social network for people who want to showcase their professional work.	**When to do it:** Once or twice a week
What you'll need: Your resume LinkedIn account A list of people who would give you recommendations 1 paragraph about how you help others, to post in your summary List of your skills,	**What to do:** Get a LinkedIn account Find people you know, connect to them Give & Get recommendations Connect your LinkedIn account to Hootsuite so you can cross-post status updates automatically. *Fill out the LinkedIn worksheets in the back of the book.*

What is LinkedIn? It's a place to advertise your business, find new business partners, learn about your competition, research someone you want to connect with, and MORE!

If you're interning or just starting your professional career, it's a place to help potential employers find out what you can do. If you're mid-career, it helps you show people how you keep learning about your field. If you're at the encore career stage, it can be a place to learn and make connections in a new industry. If you're looking to hire people, LinkedIn is a place to research what they've done, and who vouches for them.

As of this writing (February 2013), there are over 57 million people on LinkedIn in the US alone, and 11 million people on LinkedIn in India. There are over 6 million people on LinkedIn in the UK, and 4 million people on LinkedIn in Canada. And the numbers only keep growing.

But why else would you get on LinkedIn? What's the point if you're not looking for work or don't want to market your business?

LinkedIn can also be used to control the Google search results for your name. What does that mean? Have you ever been frustrated when you searched for your name online and something insignificant or worse, too revealing appeared? Or is it some random celebrity instead of you?

When you write about yourself on LinkedIn, you can control what people find out about you, and you can have a better chance of getting that next job or creating that next partnership. You are INSTANTLY easier to find, and you are in control of the message.

Now, when I search for my name, my LinkedIn profile is the second or third result down. It's useful to control my search results. And it will help you control your results too.

Let's dive in.

The internet is huge. People want to find you to hire you, give you money, learn more about you.

People want to know how you are in a business setting. You can't rely on old employers, they may not remember you, people move on, they can't speak for your record after awhile. LinkedIn is a place where you can keep all of the compliments people make. A kind of 3-D resume.

What about your privacy on LinkedIn?

This is a reasonable concern. The easier it is to learn about your previous work history, plus birthday, and college you went to, the easier it is to impersonate you. What can you do about privacy?

Well, for starters, don't list your birthday on your LinkedIn profile, even though that's an option in LinkedIn. Don't list the dates you went to school, as that can bias people against you, either for being too old or too young. Just leave those dates off.

You don't have to put dates on when you worked somewhere either.

Also, you can change your privacy settings in LinkedIn and make everything private. Go to your settings page and make sure you set your privacy clearly in these four tabs: Profile, Email Preferences, Groups, and Account. I have underlined the settings you need to edit.

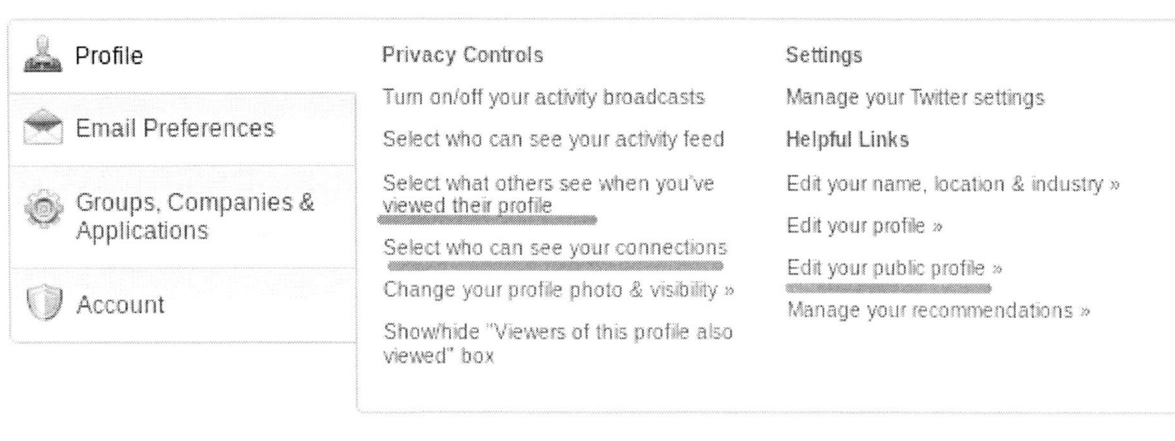

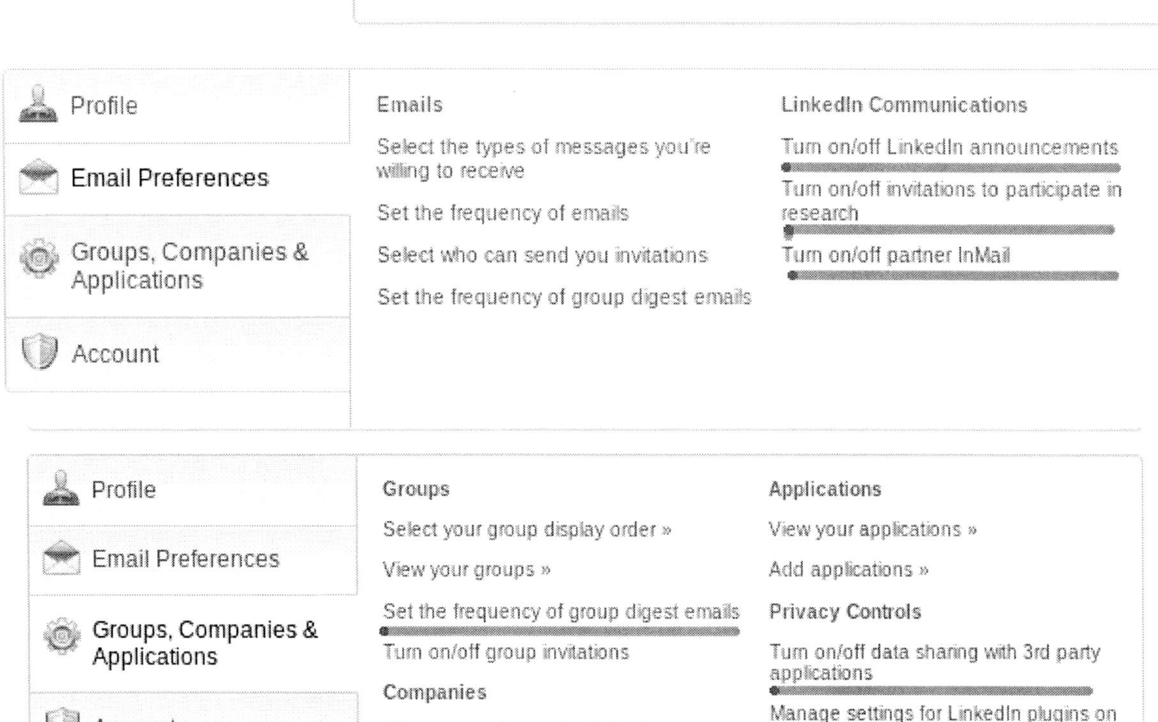

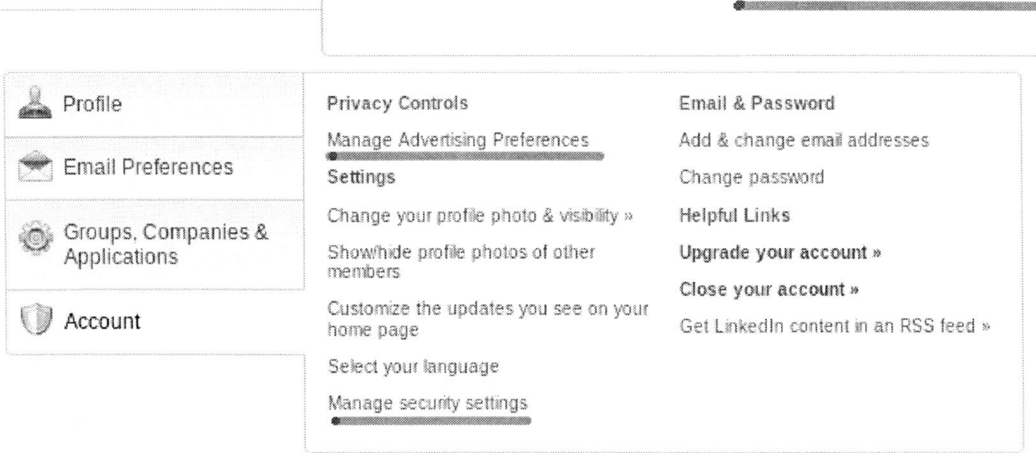

But aside from what you share on LinkedIn, how does LinkedIn share YOUR data with its advertisers? This is important because they have the power to share a lot of your personal details. Data-mining and selling data is becoming a big commodity in the internet marketing world. It is basically how Google makes billions of dollars. It works for fundraising too. In presidential elections, election teams are working with sophisticated data modeling sets to figure out who is most likely to give to their campaigns.

The rule to follow with any online social platform, whether it's Etsy, LinkedIn, Twitter or Facebook, is if there is no charge for their service, then YOU and YOUR DATA are the product.

How private IS LinkedIn? Look at Terms of Service, Didn't Read. http://tos-dr.info/. Probably when you signed up to LinkedIn, Twitter, or another site, you did not take the time to read through the entire privacy policy. This site does this for you, and highlights the problematic aspects of privacy policies on these different websites.

The good news is that on LinkedIn you can have a completely private profile, or you can choose to share more with the world. Unlike Facebook, it's professional, and you're in control of what you share. One tiny detail: If you have over 200 contacts on LinkedIn, and you want to delete your profile, you have to contact LinkedIn to get your profile removed.

If you would like to be even more private on LinkedIn, please see the LinkedIn Privacy Worksheet at the end of this book.

Creating your LinkedIn Profile

Step 1: Use Your Resume

Where have you worked in the last five years? How do you describe what you did there? Remember that good action & concrete results words go a long way. If you're stuck for action words, use these:

- Facilitated
- Directed
- Researched
- Developed
- Collaborated
- Researched

- Coordinated
- Supervised
- Wrote
- Raised

Sit down with your resume and add some previous positions. You don't have to put everything from your resume on your LinkedIn profile. Add positions relevant to where you're trying to go today.

For example, if you've worked in the insurance industry and the nonprofit world, but are now trying to get a nonprofit position, put in your volunteer jobs and board positions that you've held. If you held a job for a shorter amount of time than 6 months, leave it off. Potential employers want to see that you'll stick around.

Step 2: Your Picture

Now that you've done this, add a picture of yourself. It should be a professional-looking headshot. If you don't have one of these yet, see if you can get a friend to take a picture of you outside in the daytime. Make sure that the sun is behind the photographer. Standing in nature can be a good, neutral background.

Step 3: Your Industry

Cross-list yourself in different industries. (marketing, PR, consulting, for example). How do you do this? You have to put yourself in multiple simultaneous positions, such as saying you're a consultant 3-4 times. Each position can then be listed in a different industry, and that affects how often you'll come up in search results. If you're attempting to be hired, this can increase your chances of being found by a recruiter.

If you list your current occupation, you can cross list across industries by listing your current position several different times, with different industries. (I am listed under Nonprofit Management, Fundraising, Consulting, PR and marketing)

What do you want people to do after viewing your profile?

Do you want people to primarily see you as someone who can help them? What kind of help do you want to give? Is there something else you'd like them to buy from you or see you as? If so, list this as a concurrent job you have. Or use your headline to tell people what you want to do for them.

Step 4: Connect with people. Not everyone.

Look over your resume and remember people you've worked with.

Look them up on LinkedIn. When you connect with people, go through their contacts and see who they know. They might know some people that you know, who you'd forgotten about.

Who should you NOT connect with?

If someone tries to connect with you by using the standard LinkedIn text and saying, "I'd like to connect with you on LinkedIn" without even personalizing the greeting, just ignore it or delete them right away. Or, if you like, make it a teachable moment and message them and tell them exactly why you're not interested in connecting with them, because they didn't give you a reason why you should connect. You can also report the person as spam and say "I don't know this person."

How can you deal with connection spammers, people who just try to connect with anyone and everyone in a particular group?

Simply put, don't connect with people you don't know. A lot of people will attempt to connect with you on LinkedIn, but you should not connect with people you haven't met.

At the very least, if they want to connect with you, tell them you will have a phone-call with them, to see if there is a way you can help each other. Then, that teaches them that they are going to have to work harder to be connected to you. This is how I have gotten clients in the past. People somehow want to connect to you even more if you make it harder for them to do so.

The way I put it in my LinkedIn profile is, "*If you want to connect with me, you need to give me a reason why.*" Put it right in the top of your profile, in your summary. If the person has looked at your profile, they should have seen this part, and should attempt to make some sort of personal message to you.

LinkedIn IS a good way to meet people. I know a fantastic networker named Paul Nazareth, in Toronto Canada, who has meetings from 7-8am every week day with people he has found on LinkedIn, so he can enlarge his network. He does this because his job has lots of cubicle time, but not a lot of time out meeting people. If you keep expanding your network, who knows who you'll meet, and how you can help them, and how they can help you?

Top Tip from Paul Nazareth: Connect with 95% of people that you know, that you've met or chatted with on the phone, and 5% of people that you don't know.

You might think, “But I need lots of connections, right? I mean, more connections is a GOOD thing!” Not really. These people you've randomly connected with now have access to your personal information, and if you don't really know them, why would you give them access to that? Who knows what they'll do with it? And even if you trust them, how can you recommend their services, or connect them to others in your network without ever talking to them or knowing who they are?

It's hard to keep track of 500+ contacts. It's even hard to keep track of 200 contacts. So make your life easy and just connect with people that you have either met or spoken to. If there are some people you would like to connect with professionally, but don't know personally, then reach out to a few of them, make them that 5%, and give them a compelling reason to connect with you.

If you're reading this and have already connected with too many strangers, don't worry!

Disconnecting from people you don't know

Don't worry. They do NOT get notified if you've disconnected with them.

To remove connections, LinkedIn purposely makes it tricky. Here's how to do it. Go to your Contacts page. Click Add/Remove connections in the top right of the page.

You'll see a list of people, alphabetized by last name. Find their name, click it, and then press remove contact.

Step 5: Your Groups

In a 2012 user poll, LinkedIn found that the groups feature was people's favorite part of LinkedIn.

What is the point of being in a LinkedIn group?

You can use LinkedIn groups to connect with peers, clients, former employers, new connections, aka potential clients.

When you join a group, you've got access to everyone in that group, you can interact with them, and expand your network. You can also join a regional group to facilitate face to face meetings with people.

You can join up to 50 groups. I would advise you to join as many relevant groups as you can. If there isn't a lot of recent activity on the group, then don't bother joining it. I define recent activity as activity in the last 3 months.

When you join a group, make sure you turn off the “daily digest” or “individual email” feature because that will fill up your inbox and make you crazy. Opt to go to the group when you feel like it to get the latest news.

The other thing that LinkedIn does that slightly annoys me is that if you answer a post with a comment, you are automatically subscribed to those comments and will get a new email each time someone else comments on that post. It's better to unclick that “follow discussion” box right before you comment on a post in a group.

When you're having a workshop, talk, festival, announce it on LinkedIn groups. You can gain exposure, and people will click through to your website. When I was running a career fair for a former employer, I did my best to get the word out on LinkedIn, and the attendance swelled from 500 to 1500, and the vendors at the career fair said it was the most qualified pool of applicants they had seen in 8 years.

Step 6: Your Networks

In order to keep your profile fresh, you can add your Twitter stream. You can also choose to cross post your tweets from Hootsuite.com onto your LinkedIn Profile, without ever needing to sign in to LinkedIn.

Step 7: Get Testimonials

People believe what OTHER people say about you more than what you say about you. Actively solicit testimonials now from former or current co-workers, supervisors and clients.
Testimonials are like public compliments from people who have a connection with the work that you do. If you're interested in getting testimonials, the first thing you need to do is GIVE testimonials. So think about someone you admire. Are they on LinkedIn? Who could you say nice things about on LinkedIn?

Give a meaningful testimonial.

What is a meaningful testimonial?

Say something that this person actually did, how they did it, and what results they got. Don't just say meaningless overused adjectives like "great" "awesome" "cool" or "amazing." Pick up your thesaurus and get creative.

Remember when you give a testimonial to have your thesaurus handy. You don't want to just write "This person is a good worker and I was happy to work with them." You want to write something that will tell the reader a few interesting facts about this person, maybe a little story that illustrates why they are so good to work with. Here's a testimonial that I wrote, a bit tongue in cheek, but there are so many boring LinkedIn recommendations out there. Make yours memorable.

"Pataphysical investigation is not for the meek. It takes strength of character, a devotion to scholarship, and a deep curiosity about the world. From an evolutionary standpoint, Mr. Havelka has surpassed these qualifications. He is a farseeing initiator, handy with deep philosophical texts, a buoyant and productive leader. Since his howling success in Aristotelian logic, Slavic linguistics, violin virtuosity and world traveling, we wonder, what will he do for an encore? Well, he's currently producing a "brick engine" which will make elephant-hide pahoehoe into hairstone. He was instrumental in the rediscovery of the 8th century Arabic alembics used to create both acids and perfumes. In

short, he's a wonder worker who can call spirits from the vasty deep. (He does disembodied visits by request)"

If your testimonial makes the person reading it smile, you've guaranteed that they will be more likely to remember it, and think of your friend when they need someone.

And the nice thing is, the more meaningful testimonials you give out, the more you get. You can even write the testimonial for someone when you request a testimonial, to make it even easier for them to recommend you (they have the option to edit it of course).

Whenever you meet new people and do work for them, volunteer or pro bono or otherwise, get testimonials.

If appropriate, find former clients on there, and connect with them, and get testimonials.

Starting your own LinkedIn Group

Why would you start your own LinkedIn Group? If you want

- More attention for your business
- Another place to post your blog posts
- To tell people about special deals on your products or services
- To create a community of potential customers, or
- To poll people to ask them what they want to learn more about

Then you might benefit from creating a LinkedIn Group.

Before you create a LinkedIn group, look and see if there's another group that is already talking about your main niche. Who is active in this space? Which LinkedIn groups have become dormant? Is there a way that you can ask people in the dormant group to come and join your group?

Should it be an open or closed group?

It's up to you. Open groups are good because then you'll get more people joining with less work for you. However, closed groups that people have to apply to join have been shown to make potential members value the group membership more.

Use Polls in your group

If you use a poll, you'll be able to find out what people's goals, agendas, and pains are, and then their answers can help you write a sales page, create a product, or speak directly to what your potential customers want to accomplish.

Give discounts and beta access to your group members

This will help your group members feel special. Give them discounts, or give them access to a private beta version of your new website. Ask them to test things for you, or tell you what they think about the cost of your products. Too low? Too high? Just right? Here's where you can test drive aspects of your business before putting them out in the world.

Call someone from your group once a week, just to say hi. This will help you build a relationship with them, and it will set you apart as a group that truly cares about the well-being of its members.

Recent Changes to LinkedIn, as of February 2013

- LinkedIn has taken away Answers, Slideshare widget and Amazon Reading widgets.
- LinkedIn has changed the color scheme to a darker scheme,
- They've put a flag at the top of the page to show you if there has been activity on something you've posted or commented on.
- They also have changed the message box to have a little red indicator showing how many people have messaged you or want to connect with you.
- They've changed your skill section so that it becomes a place where people can "endorse" you for a skill you claim to have. I see 2 problems with this. One is that it enables them to gather more information about you. The second problem is that an endorsement for a skill doesn't really mean anything. It isn't a letter of reference or a testimonial. It's just another way to waste time on LinkedIn.
- LinkedIn used to automatically post your Tweets to your LinkedIn timeline if your Twitter profile was connected to your LinkedIn profile. This year that will no longer happen, so if you want to auto-post your tweets to your LinkedIn timeline, you need to use a service like Hootsuite.com.

What did you learn?

- How to get testimonials
- How to list yourself in different industries and get more profile views.
- Cross post your updates with Hootsuite.com to keep your LinkedIn profile "fresh"

Take Action:

- Who is someone you could ask right now for a testimonial on LinkedIn?
- What could you call your group?
- What are some groups you could join?

LinkedIn Must Know

- Your profile is your face. You need a flattering professional photograph.
- Giving testimonials will lead to you getting testimonials.
- Your headline is your mission. Is it telling the world who you are?

LinkedIn Must Do

- Connect with your friends and former colleagues on LinkedIn.
- Join 5 groups related to your industry and what you're looking for.
- Give a testimonial
- Reach out and have a phone call or coffee with someone from LinkedIn
- *Fill out the LinkedIn worksheets in the back of the book.*

Chapter 6.5: Tweet your way to the Top

What is it? Twitter.com is a powerful platform to create friends and market your stuff. It's kind of a chat for the entire world. No matter what language you speak or where you want to sell things, you can find your audience on here.	**When to do it** Every day for 15 minutes
What you'll need A picture of yourself A Twitter handle that reflects who you are (like your name) or what you do (like your profession or business name) Hootsuite account Tweetbig account or Sprout-Social account List of hashtag chats for your field, go here to find http://bit.ly/TwitterChatMaster	**What to do:** Create a Twitter account Create a Hootsuite account, link the Twitter account to it. Put in your custom background. Start conversations with people by retweeting their blog posts, asking them questions, participating in hashtag chats. Do a search to see the top influencers in your niche. Follow these people, retweet them, and mention them, ask for their advice. *Fill out the Twitter worksheets in the back of the book.*

What's the point of Twitter exactly? Why DO it?

Have you ever wanted to be in the know? Have you ever wanted a way to discover new technologies in your industry, or breaking news in the world?

One night in early May 2011, I saw this status update on Twitter from journalist @BrianStelter. It said, "Our sources say that Osama Bin Laden is dead." I thought, "No way, surely the New York Times and the Huffington Post would be all over this by now if this were true" but I scanned their sites and saw nothing.

A few hours later, the status updates continued, and said, "No, really, Osama bin Laden is dead." Then the news outlets started to talk about it. Even if the news outlets knew before it was released, this news broke on Twitter. I felt privileged to have been there at that moment when it seemed like tech-heads who used Twitter knew something and posted it even before big media outlets posted something about it.

You'd think, for someone who was in New York City during the 9/11 attacks, that this killing would mean something. It does mean something, but not a revenge. It means, for me, the little epiphany that Twitter *can be an accurate and useful source of news*, even if it is, as tech journalist Tom Foremski says, a re-distribution of mass media. He writes on his blog,

> *"Social media has largely become Social Distribution Of Mass Media, aka SoDOMM"*[*]

Be that as it may, when you look at protests around the world in the last couple of years, whether in Egypt in 2011 or Iran in 2009, Twitter has been a powerful tool to help people organize and coordinate their movements, local news for people who need to know, not just national news. We MAKE the news when we use Twitter.

My Story

Here's my story on how Twitter has been incredibly powerful for me. In 2010 I connected with @PamelaGrow on Twitter. She lives in Pennsylvania. I lived in Texas. It was unlikely that we would have ever met. She started to retweet me, and I started to retweet her, and then she suggested that we have a phone-call. It turned out that we had a lot in common. We loved fundraising for nonprofits, we were both consultants starting to be more active on Twitter, and she asked me to

---

* http://www.siliconvalleywatcher.com/mt/archives/2011/05/mediawatch_bin.php

be a guest on her Twitter chat, #smNPchat. After that, we started to have a call every month just to check in with each other. I wrote a couple of guest posts on her blog.

She recommended that I ask someone on Twitter to do a guest post on About.com, and I did this, and got a lot more traffic because of it.

One month in 2011, she mentioned that she was going to start doing webinars with a webinar company. Then in May I contacted this company and by July I was making $2,000+ a month with the company.

Because of my friendship with Pam, started on Twitter, I was able to get not just webinars but actual in-person speaking engagements with nonprofits across the country who came to my webinars. I spoke for Meals on Wheels national webinars in June 2012, and they also asked me to speak at their national conference. I spoke at the Scleroderma Foundation national leadership conference in July 2012, and they asked me to do webinars for them as well. Since that time I've also been able to send some speaking engagements Pam's way, to help start to repay her for all that she's done for me. We have actually met in person and talked on the phone a lot, and it's always been a blast. She's exactly the same in person as she is online.

Recently Pam decided to start a mastermind group and she asked me to help her lead it. She asked some of the best people in the nonprofit consulting space to be in this group, and many people said yes. Since starting that group, we have had a call just about every month, and we've covered topics such as self-publishing, how to manage a product launch, how to manage affiliates, membership sites, and more. I am the youngest person in this group, and everyone else has more experience than I do, and I am learning so much.

As you can see, connecting with this one person has led to a world of opportunity for me. And this is just one story from the many exciting people I have met on Twitter.

Who should you follow? Should you automatically follow back?

No. Don't auto-follow people. Success on Twitter is not about who has the most followers. Having lots of followers is nice, but having real relationships with people who follow you is even better.

If a bunch of random people start to follow you, even if they have 25,000 followers, don't be flattered. What will happen is they think you'll automatically follow them back, and then once you do, after a week they'll unfollow you. They just want to game the system and look popular, and they will never listen or engage with you, so why bother following them?

Followers versus relationships

Should you go for number of followers or should you go for deep relationships?

Honestly, I would take a little from column A, and a little from column B. Because you are only one person, you can't go for lots of followers and expect to have deep relationships with all of them. Trying to keep up too many relationships would make you crazy. So what I usually do is try to follow 500-1,000 people, but have conversations with only a handful of people, maybe 20-30 people, ideally influencers, and people who seem most responsive. What most responsive means is people who will follow me back, retweet me, and have @mention conversations with me.

What about privacy on Twitter?

If you've already signed up for Twitter, you probably didn't wade through the privacy policy. Almost no one does. Solution? If you go to http://tos-dr.info, or Terms of Service, Didn't Read, you'll see a small version of what Twitter is doing with its privacy policy. It's a bit better than Facebook, which is not saying much I know, but fair is fair.

You can make your tweets “protected” which will put a lock on your Twitter account so the only people who can follow you are people you personally approve.
If you want to do business and find customers on Twitter, I'd choose not to do this option, but if you're seriously concerned about privacy, it can make Twitter less scary.

It's true that the Library of Congress is keeping track of all of our tweets. That's kind of scary, but since we're in total control of what we share, we shouldn't worry unduly about that. Your Twitter profile is not going to be like a Facebook profile, which can say your birth date, your school, and link to your entire family as well as show everyone your location. You're not required to use your real name, like you are on Google+. Your Twitter profile can be as anonymous as you like. You can share your location or not.

Top tip. Don't "check in" with location services unless you want everyone to know where you go and what you do.

What about ads?

To opt out of the promoted tweets on Twitter, you want to install the Stylish Firefox extension, then go to http://UserStyles.org and find a Stylish Ad-On that blocks promoted tweets in Hootsuite. They may make one that blocks tweets on Twitter as well, so check back there periodically.

What about emails?

So it used to be that Twitter would NEVER email you. Now they have decided that they're going to create new email preferences without telling people, and automatically check your preferences for you, which sucks because who needs more emails? These emails include "Advertise on Twitter!" emails and "People You may Know" and "Daily Digest" from Twitter. Ugh. If you want to opt out of Twitter's increasingly annoying emails, just go to the little "gear" icon on the top right. Then go to Email Notifications

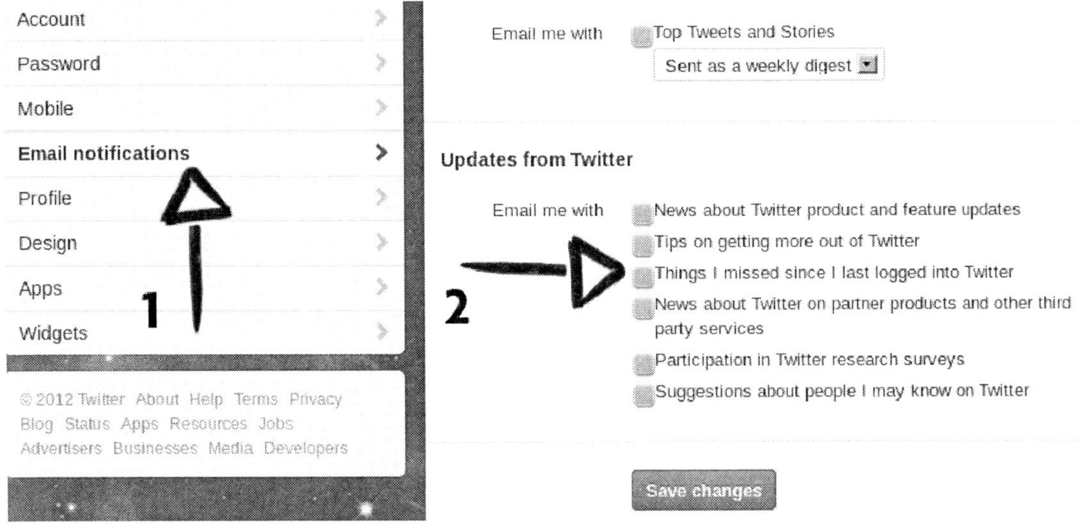

Then un-check all of the "Updates from Twitter." I've shown you what that looks like above.

Let's get into how to use Twitter. Here's Twitter 101

1. Research who in your field has a lot of followers with the internal Twitter search or TweetBig.com (For example, your field might be Beer, Health care, Marketing, Accounting, Leadership, etc)

These people who have a lot of followers, we call influencers.

These are people who have influence within Twitter because having lots of followers means lots of people think what you say is worthwhile.

And when influencers mention you in Twitter, you will find a lot of people looking up your website, and potentially following you too.

2. Start with following the influencer.
Sometimes influencers will only follow a few people who they admire. If this the case, it might be a good idea to look at those people too, and see if they are also influencers (aka have lots of followers).

3. If they follow you back, say thank you.
Example: @wildwomanfund, thank you for following me! I love your blog!

4. Mention them and ask them a question related to your site.
Example: @mindy, what is the best way to get Twitter traffic back to my site?

5. What is retweeting and why do you do it?
Retweeting is when you help someone on Twitter get more exposure for their ideas. This is also known as "amplification."

When you retweet someone's tweet, all of your followers can see this tweet now and it's credited back to the original person who wrote it.

You can retweet someone by putting your cursor over the bottom of the message, and it will give you the option to say Retweet or Reply.

You can also type "RT" which means Retweet, and then the person's twitter handle, like "@jessica_journey" and then the message. This will show up to the person more readily than a retweet, which makes them remember you more.

6. *Retweet the influencer.*
Example: LOL This>> RT @sasha says: "CLEAN ALL THE THINGS!"

7. When you mention the influencer, put a "@" symbol, and then their Twitter handle. You can have conversations with them this way. If you have written something they might enjoy, you can then put a link in which links back to your site. Since Twitter makes it difficult to write a long website address, put your address, or "URL" into a URL shortener, such as http://bit.ly.

8. *What is a list, and why is it useful?*
A list is a way to organize people you are interested in keeping track of on Twitter.

When you look right above your "home feed" on Twitter (below where you type in a message), you can see a little gear button. Click on this button and it will give you the option to create a list.

When you create a list, you can name it something complimentary, such as "Fabulous people I talk with" or "Useful Information on <YourField>."

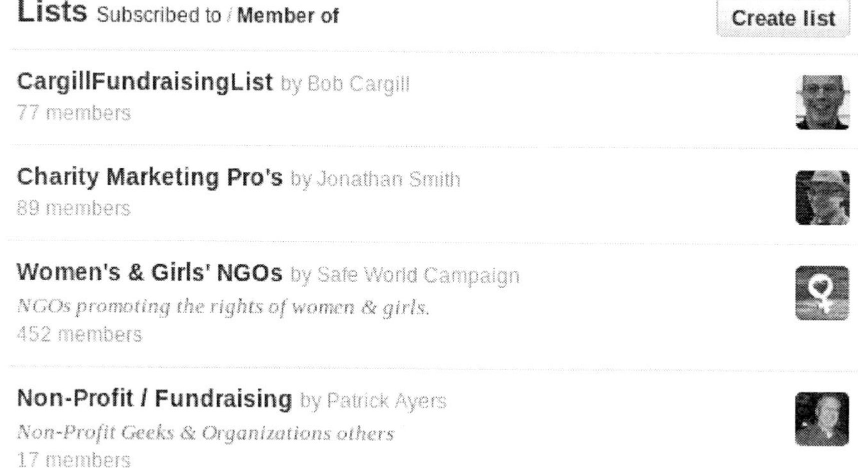

When you put someone on a list, they will notice you have done so, and they might also put you on a list of their own. The lists they make will help more people be aware of you and see you as an influencer too.

What should you tweet about?

Share with others!

- Post what you're doing, such as teaching, blog posts, events, etc.
- Put out a call for information.
- Share your knowledge and start to build relationships.

Twitter intermediate strategies: How to build relationships?

What if you just want to find customers or donors?

If you just want to have conversations with your potential customers and do customer service for current ones, Twitter is a powerful tool to do this. It's a place to answer people's concerns, manage your reputation and find new people who want to listen to you and buy from you. I have made sales through Twitter, and as far as I can see, most companies use it for customer service, as Twitter is often the place people will take their complaints.

It helps if you think about it this way. We used to curry favor with major media networks, ask and plead and cajole to get some airtime with our press releases. But now?

We are all broadcast networks now, and Twitter allows us to broadcast to a specific segment of people who care about what we care about.

Radio, newspapers, TV and other forms of "push marketing" cannot promise such a specific segment of humanity. I recently talked with a guy who paid $15,000 for a five minute TV spot, and he said it didn't even impact his website traffic stats, let alone sell anything.

When we use social media, we get the chance to talk with our EXACT target audience every single day, because they have given us their permission. People who follow you have voluntarily agreed to listen to you. They are much more likely to care due to their choice. And they are much more likely to talk with you.

For example, a person I listen to a lot on Twitter is Umair Haque

(@umairh). He writes for the Harvard Business Review, he has snarky tweets about economics, and has tons of followers. However he really does listen and talk back to his followers. This makes me listen to him, retweet him, and write blog posts about what he says.

If you want to sell your products or services or get donations through Twitter, you want influential people to talk about your products and services. How can you get them to do that?

1. Find influencers by searching for your keywords in the Twitter search bar.
2. Send an @ mention
3. Retweet them
4. Follow back
5. Have a conversation

<u>Goals for Twitter relationships</u>
Get people to retweet
Get people to write blog posts
Get talked about

If you can get this next equation, you can get what this chapter is about.

Building relationships with mentions, retweets, and chats + Reaching out with phone calls = Connecting with Influencers and getting money from these relationships

The big picture goal is how to get people on Twitter to do what you want. And for this, you don't necessarily have to have a lot of followers. Much like with LinkedIn, you don't want to have to go crazy trying to keep track of all of the people that you're following.

1. Notice other people

Retweet people, and then just mention them, show them you are interested in them. Tell your followers to follow them.

2. Appreciate other people

Show people you are listening and that you like them, by saying. “Good idea!” or “I never thought of that!” or “Useful article by @wildwomanfund”. Thank them when they mention you too.

3. Encourage Dialogue.

@ mention them on Twitter, (like "Hey @amandahess, I love your column for the Washington Post!") and to take it one step further, jump into hashtag chats with people. Your dialogue with them will go far towards helping them know, like, and trust you. For every pronouncement you make on Twitter, see if you can ask 2 questions.

4. Ask them to do something for you.
For example: Direct Message: "Hi @AlexandraT, I don't want to be too forward, but would you be interested in guest blogging for me? :)"

Direct Message: "I'm interested in biotech and social media, we should chat! :)"

Direct Message: "Hi! would you be open to chatting via phone or Skype one day next week? I would love to learn more about what you're doing."

@Mention. "Hey @ElizabethMinnow, what do you think of this post? http://bit.ly/ty Would you comment on it?"

Speaking of dialogue, I met three of my current business partners through Twitter, all because they reached out to me. For example, Desiree Adaway, a nonprofit career coach and former Senior Director of Volunteer Mobilization at Habitat for Humanity, connected with me and said, "Hey, let's talk!" So we got on the phone, and inside of ten minutes we were laughing like old friends. We both knew the realities of the nonprofit world, the long hours, the lonely job hunt, the wish for things to be different.

In a pause in the conversation, Desiree said, "I'd love to interview you about your journey and record it for my coaching program."

I said, "Delighted to! How about next week?

Desiree said, "Marvelous! And if I can do anything for you..."

I said, "Well, I would love to have you do a guest blog post on my website!"

And so it happened.

We kept in contact, and a few months after that call, we decided to do a joint launch of our products with a couple of friends. Our launch was successful, and we all enjoyed the feeling of helping others while making money on our own terms.

I have to confess, I was skeptical as to the use of Twitter in the beginning, but now I know so many wonderful people through it, and it has become such an important tool to have conversations with, and I would not want to run a business without it.

Advanced TWITTER!

What is a hashtag chat? It's a Party! You're INVITED!

What is it? A hashtag chat is a place where you can freely ask and answer questions about the subject of the chat, using a hashtag to help people find you in their Twitter stream. (example hashtags for the chat would include: #smNPchat, #cartalk4, #i<3tupperware, or anything you want)

Where? On Twitter! Go here to find a constantly updated Google doc spreadsheet with lists of different hashtag chats: http://bit.ly/ChatSched

Who is this for? Your followers, anyone on Twitter who might join in, and their followers too!

When? Whenever you have 5 influencers ready to engage!

An influencer could mean, for example, people with at least 2,000 Twitter followers who tend to blog and tweet about what your website is mainly about.

If it's beer, they're beer bloggers. If it's advertising, they're advertising bloggers.

Should you start having your own hashtag chats? There are no hard and fast rules about this. Theoretically, you could set up a hashtag chat right now, and just start chatting with anyone who came along.

However, you'd have a much greater chance of success if you announced it to your list, gave them at least 5 days notice, and started tweeting notices about the hashtag chat every day, and then the hour before, 15 minutes before, and 5 minutes before it was supposed to start.

You'd ALSO increase your chances of success with a hashtag chat if you have an FAQ about your chat, what the past and upcoming topics are, who you'll interview on the chat, and of course when it is, and how people can participate. Pamela Grow has done an excellent job of laying out how to participate in her tweet chats here: http://www.pamelasgrantwritingblog.com/1941/smnpchat-are-you-participating/

Hashtag chats
Make sure you have at least 500 followers and started to touch the influencers at least ten times before asking them to participate in your hashtag chat.

Twitter search engines for Twitter chats
Some of the search engines I've used and like are; Twitterfall, TweetGrid and Tweetchat. Twitter chats can be fast and furious so just watch a few before diving in.

Top Tip!
When you follow people on Twitter, make a list of bloggers who seem influential in your niche, then go to their blogs and set up RSS feeds for their blogs, so when you comment on their blogs, you can tell them on Twitter, and invite them to visit your site or engage in a discussion with you. You can also use Twylah or Tweetbig to find the influencers.

How to do a custom Twitter background
Twitter keeps changing its look so I have no advice about creating your own custom Twitter backgrounds. However, if you Google the phrase "how to create custom Twitter backgrounds," you'll be able to find graphic designer blogs where they'll tell you the exact pixel measurements to use. There are a few services that will make them for you too, such as http://Twitbacks.com or Themeleon at http://Colourlovers.com/themeleon/twitter.

My favorite Twitter tool
http://Hootsuite.com is my favorite tool, and it's free for up to 5 accounts. Hootsuite allows you to schedule tweets weeks or months in advance. For more detail on this, see the worksheets in the back of the book.

How to get more followers fast.

If you want a lot of followers fast, use http://TweetBig.com, a tool allowing you to find the influencers in your niche quickly, and also to find people to follow you back automatically, which will allow you to follow even more people, and expand your reach. Tweetbig costs $18 per month, but in my opinion, it's worth it.

Other useful Twitter tools

I like Twitter Counter. You can go to http://twittercounter.com to get a widget to put on the side of your blog. This shows you who comes to your website from Twitter. People can see their own pictures on your site, and this subtly influences them to come back.

TweetSmarter is so useful. Check this out. Below you'll see people who responded to one question I asked on Twitter. I had no idea who these people were, and had never connected with any of them before. Over 50 people ended up responding to my question. It was heartwarming and completely unexpected.

All I did was say,

“Hey Twitter, can you help me? I am looking for small clinics and rural hospitals who are using social media.”

WissingerPhotog Wissinger Photo
@wildwomanfund not small, but maybe a lead w @ScrippsHealth
30 minutes ago

itswendylou itswendylou
@wildwomanfund I know they're not small but @MissionAVL tweets
31 minutes ago

JooLeeV Julie Verdes
@wildwomanfund @concentrahealth is pretty active on social media
31 minutes ago

Samjb Samra Bufkins MJ,APR
RT @wildwomanfund: Hey Twitter, can you help me? I'm looking for examples of small #hospitals and #clinics using #SocialMedia
32 minutes ago

AdInfinitum Dan Dashnaw
@wildwomanfund Here's a shared Google spreadsheet that lists a ton of hospitals and their social URLs: http://j.mp/fcDF3L
33 minutes ago

These are just some of the over 25 answers I received. Ask Twitter a question or ask TweetSmarter to help you, and who knows? You just might get some useful and unusual answers, using the wisdom of Twitter users all over the world!

Recent Changes to Twitter, as of October 2012

- Twitter has started showing previews of videos if you link a video, to keep people on Twitter instead of clicking away to another service.
- Twitter has started showing previews of pictures, for the same reason.
- Twitter has put "TwitPics" underneath your profile picture on the left-hand side of the screen.
- Twitter has changed the design of a person's Twitter page again, so that some people are opting to have a larger picture at the top of their Twitter Profile.
- Twitter has changed its policy around emailing users, so you may get an email or two or three asking you if you want to advertise

on Twitter.

- Twitter has promoted Tweets and promoted hashtags, but you don't have to look at promoted tweets if you install a Stylish add-on to block them.
- LinkedIn used to automatically post your Tweets to your LinkedIn timeline if your Twitter profile was connected to your LinkedIn profile. That is no longer happening, so if you want to auto-post your tweets to your LinkedIn timeline, you need to use a service like http://Hootsuite.com.

Twitter keeps changing so please go and see for yourself before just assuming that everything in this book still holds true.

These new changes, in my opinion, do nothing for the Twitter experience, and degrade the Twitter screen, making it even more cluttered, and even more difficult to pay attention to people on Twitter. Every social network has a certain shelf-life, and no one knows how long that shelf life is. Therefore, even though I love Twitter, don't depend too much on one social media platform for your business, not even this one.

Remember!

For more meaningful Twitter conversation

- Research your keywords and start to follow people who frequently use them.
- Mention these people and ask them questions, comment on their blog posts. Participate in Twitter Chats with specialized hashtags.
- Research the top influencers in your niche and mention, retweet them frequently.

Build Social Capital & Conversions

- Get known as a person who will retweet, and who thanks people. People remember this, and will go back and look for things you've said to retweet to their own followers. You can exponentially expand your reach in a few months.
- Use your Twitter traffic to drive people to your website, where they can sign up for your newsletter, and then you can sell them your products and services (this is conversions).
- Use your Twitter relationships to create products with your new Twitter friends, or create affiliate marketing relationships with them.

Twitter Must Know

- Don't follow everyone.
- Don't just auto-tweet your blog posts.
- Reach out and mention new people each week

Twitter Must Do

- Make sure to un-check your "email notifications" so you don't get inundated with emails.
- Follow people who have interesting things to say.
- Let your tweets be useful & funny & link back to your blog.
- Read *The Tao of Twitter"* by @markwschaefer (Mark Schaefer)
- *Fill out the Twitter worksheets in the back of the book.*

Chapter 6.6: Gonna be okay, just comment (and dance)

What is it? Blog comments are a way to get people to find you, as well as an SEO tool to help Google rank your site higher in the search results. You will find traffic to your website increases EVERY TIME if you follow the steps below.	**When to do it:** Every night, right before you go to sleep
What you'll need: A blog A Netvibes account A URL shortener SEOBook in your Firefox toolbar Some time late at night to comment on blogs	**What to do:** Comment on blogs Create articles on other websites that link back to your blog Guest post on other blogs Retweet your articles on Twitter and LinkedIn *Fill out the Commenting worksheets in the back of the book.*

Problem! Nobody knows about you, your blog, or who you are.

You need to create relationships with people in your niche. You also need to build backlinks to your site to come up higher in search engine results. AND you want to drive people who are looking at your competitors to your site.

Solution!

Commenting on other people's websites happily combines all of these goals into one series of actions. Namely, commenting every night on different blogs in your niche.

How do you find blogs to comment on?

Comment on the blogs you find most interesting, and also on blogs with the most incoming links. You can start to find these blogs by going to http://alltop.com and looking to see if there is a category for your niche. If there is, see who is listed there. Also, do an internet search for the keywords for your niche and the word blog and see what comes up. Do a search for a typical question in your industry. You can find websites people go to frequently for answers to their questions.

How can you find out which blogs have the most incoming links?

Install SEOBook.com's toolbar for your Firefox browser. Just go to http://SEOBook.com and sign up. Then you'll be able to see how many incoming links the website has. Here's what it looks like.

There are lots of different numbers in the SEOBook toolbar, and I like to look at the MajesticSEO number of links (circled above), as well as the age of the site. There is a big audience if there are a lot of incoming links. A big audience means a lot of people will click on through to your website if you make a useful and thoughtful comment.

What makes a good comment?

Something 2-3 paragraphs long that shows that you really thought about the article, and also, that you took into account other commenters' view points. Don't just skip to the end (unless there are tons of comments). If there are 10 or fewer comments, take some time to see what other people thought.

For example, let's say you've written a long post about how to increase your blog readership. I have something to add to that. I might write:

"Dear Blog post writer,

Thank you so much for writing about getting more readers. It's not just about posting a lot though, it's about writing in a compelling way. And the only way to write better is to practice! I started out writing blog posts 5 days a week, and now I've gone to 2 days a week. I do a weekly e-newsletter though, which really helps people come back and read my blog.

Another thing I like to do is pick out pithy and illuminating sentences out of my blog post, and shorten the URL, and set up those sentences in Hootsuite for my Twitter and LinkedIn accounts, especially in the morning. I've found that scheduling my updates for the morning, during the week, is the best.

I'm definitely going to try a couple of the methods you suggested though. This was helpful. Thanks again!

Mazarine"

Do you see how I offered two ways to build blog readership? And how I complimented the author as well? This is a good way to get people to see that you have something useful to say. With some blog commenting systems, you can enter your URL and people can click your name and go directly to your website, or if you have a relevant blog article about the subject, you can link to that at the end of your comment as well. If you have a post related to the post you are commenting on, you could write, "*I would like to continue the conversation here:* ***http://bit.ly/ty"*** and link to your RELEVANT post.

Here's another example of a good comment.

This comment is in response to an article about universities trying to make nonprofit MBA programs. The post finished up with some resources people could use to do proper HR practices, as most nonprofits do not have an HR person. I wrote:

"Thanks for helping people feel a bit better about these tricky HR pieces of the nonprofit world. A lot of nonprofits could be more effective if they followed proper hiring and firing practices. I used to work with an orchestra board that thought if someone played a musical instrument, that was a good enough job qualification to be marketing director.

Thanks again for writing this.

Mazarine"

Here's another, shorter comment, based on a blog post at http://ReadWriteWeb.com. This blog post was an infographic about when it's best to send emails.

"I send a lot of emails and I've tried sending them at different times of day, and different days of the week. This infographic confirms my own experience, that the majority of times people open emails is between 8-9am on a weekday.

Thanks for sharing this fun infographic!

Mazarine
http://wildsocialmedia.com"

Remember, when you start to comment, don't just say "Nice post." Say, "Dear <name of blog writer> and then a thoughtful opinion on their post, whether agreeing or disagreeing. Sign off with "Sincerely" or another respectful sign off, and put your name at the bottom. If you've really gotten into the whole comment process, and you've written something longer, consider copy-pasting your comment and making a whole blog post about it, linking back to the blog post that inspired you, and creating good will with that blogger.

How can you keep track of the blogs you want to comment on?

Use an RSS Feed Reader. Wha?

What is an RSS feed?** RSS stands for Really Simple Syndication. This means that you can save any search you do online, such as Craigslist searches, SimplyHired.com, Google searches, and more. You can also save news websites, blogs, humor sites, whatever you like, as long as they have feeds. A feed can be delineated with an orange symbol like the one on the right.

If you can't find the feed link on the website itself, then you can search for the website name plus the word "RSS feed."

** http://en.wikipedia.org/wiki/RSS

If you want to save a RSS feed for a Wordpress blog, try the name of the blog plus the word feed, at the end. So, for example: http://wildsocialmedia.com becomes http://wildsocialmedia.com/feed.

What is an RSS feed reader? An RSS Feed Reader is a place you can keep all of your internet searches saved, as well as a place to check your social networks, or your email if you like.

How do you use an RSS feed? Let's walk through it, step by step.

Step 1. Create an account on http://netvibes.com and log in.

Step 2. Find a blog you would like to follow. Here are several ways to find blogs.

- Think about who you admire in your field. Do they have a blog? Do an RSS feed for their blog.

- Research different keywords in your niche, set up Google alerts or social mention alerts for keywords.

- Research blogs in your niche, using http://alltop.com, as well as Twitter influencers you follow, as well as using a Google search for bloggers in your niche.

Step 3. Add the blogs which seem to be influential to your Netvibes RSS reader. How do you do this?

Go to the different blogs and find the RSS feed.

Step 4. Go back to your http://Netvibes.com page and click on the big green button on the top left that says Add Content.

Step 5. Go to the Orange button that says “Add a feed”

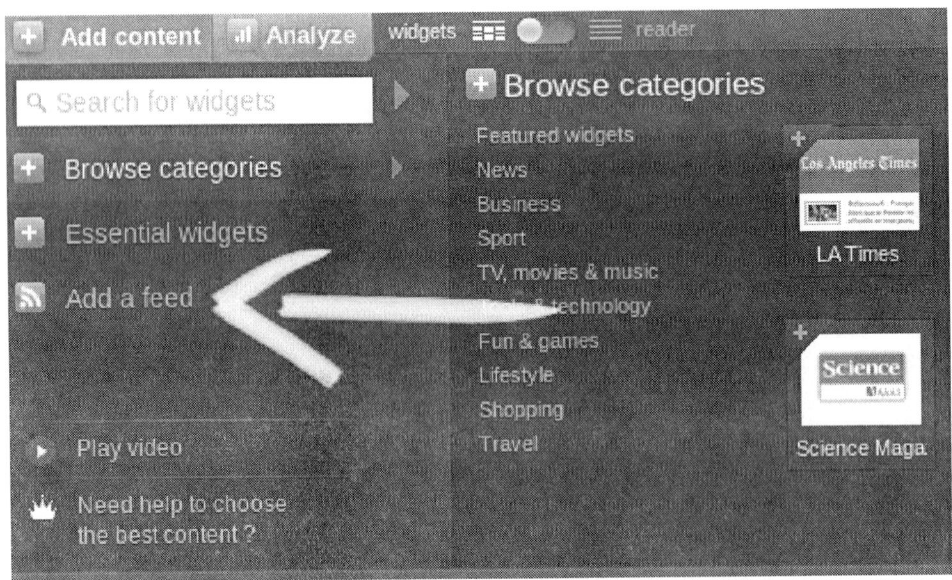

Step 6. Add the feed address, for example add http://wildsocialmedia.com/feed in the white box, then click Add feed.

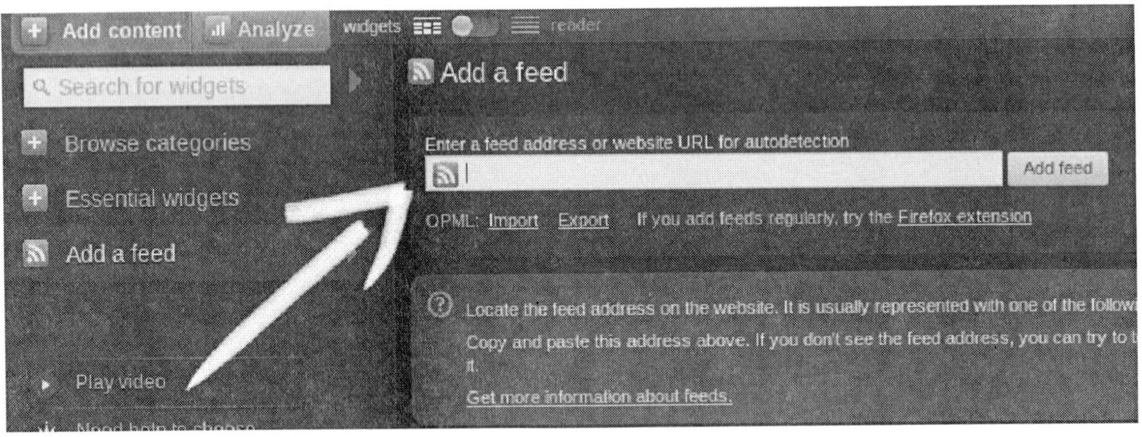

Step 7. If the feed is a valid feed, aka if you've typed it in correctly, and if the feed actually exists, you'll see a little grey box with the name of the feed underneath the white box, which you can drag down to your tabs. This saves the search or feed as long as you want.

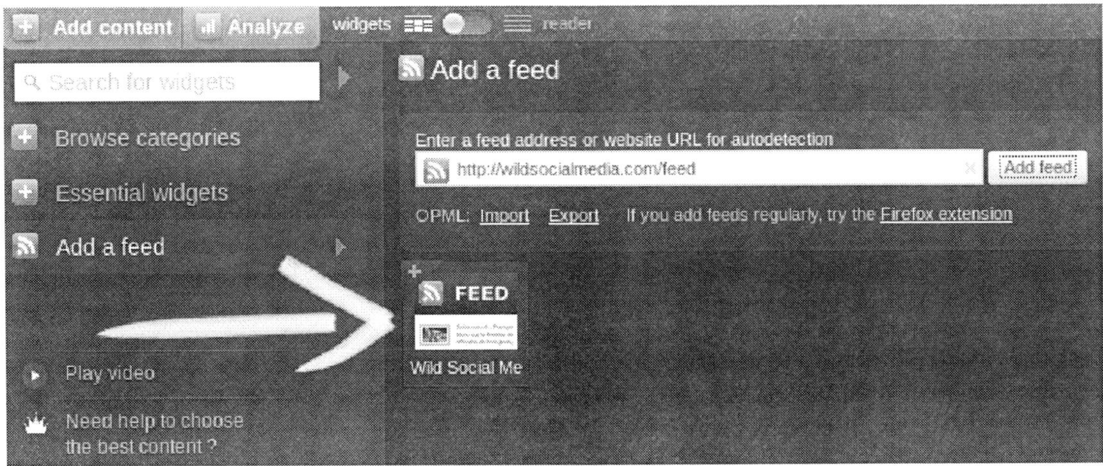

Top Tip! Put blogs for certain topics under their own tab. For example, if you're a fundraising blogger AND a philanthropy blogger, put these in two separate tabs. Also, make a tab for jokes. Because it's good to laugh as much as you can!

If you've just started blogging, you may not have a lot of posts up yet, but looking at what people are talking about can give you ideas for posts. So these feeds can help you start to make a little idea file of things you'd like to address or write a contrasting opinion to.

Once you've read 3-4 blogs, see if you can find some RECENT articles you'd like to comment on. I'd say if the article is more than a month old, don't bother. Open up all of your blogs in tabs in your browser, and start to comment. I like to comment at 10pm at night, when the rest of the work for the day is done.

If you have time, comment on three to ten blogs per night. Only comment on meaningful, interesting, or useful articles. Don't force yourself to comment on boring blogs. It will come across in the comment. Put your website under your name at the bottom of the comment. This will increase your incoming links.

Top Tips for Commenting:
Be Relevant, Include a useful link, and use Netvibes to track the blogs you want to comment on.

The best comments are relevant because you

- Read the article fully.
- Respond in a thoughtful, meaningful way. 1-3 paragraphs is good.

- Respectfully disagree if you need to, always keep it clean.

Commenting is good because

- It will drive conversation to your site.
- It will also drive people who are simply looking for more information on how to solve a problem.
- It will show people that you have thought deeply about this subject, and will make them more inclined to consider you a leader.

Top Netvibes Tips

- Create tabbed RSS searches for each specific topic in your niche. Get 10-100 frequently updated blogs in your niche to follow.
- You can comment on several sites consistently, or you can spread your comments around. Either way works.
- You can create Google alerts (here's how to set up a Google alert: http://google.com/alerts) and set them up as Netvibes feeds when people mention your keywords. This can lead you to new sources of buyers or clients, and help you stay on top of the latest developments in your topic area.

Must Know

- Comments help build your site's search engine credibility.
- Comments help potential customers find your website.
- Comments help establish your reputation as someone with useful advice.

Must Do

- Use Netvibes to keep track of different blogs you want to comment on
- Comment on 10 blogs per night
- Make a relevant comment each time, and link back to a post if you have one.
- Fill out the Commenting worksheets in the back of the book.

Chapter 7: Communicating Results - Which Metrics Matter?

What is it? Marketing online can be a lonely business. How do you know you're making any traction at all? And if you have a boss, how can you show results?	**When to do it:** Weekly during a campaign and Monthly otherwise
What you'll need: Look at Ken Burbary's wiki http://wiki.kenburbary.com I use: SproutSocial Tweetbig TweetReach TwitterGrader Hubspot blog grader Google analytics Webalizer	**What to do:** Establish a baseline; where you are now. Figure out where you want to be. Remember there is no ROI of a relationship. You just have to build them. Familiarize yourself with the metric tools. Find the ones that suit you. *Fill out the Metrics worksheets in the back of the book.*

"*Social media is the culmination of marketing, customer service and communications in real time in front of everyone. Any tool that affords you to do so much and reach so many people for free cannot be summed up with one simple measurement.*" - Eve Mayer Osburn, *Social Media for the CEO*

Problem! Too Much DATA!

Did you know that there are over 1.9 billion people online? And this number is only going to grow by 2020. There are over 5 million terabytes of data on the internet. To give you an idea of how big that is, Google's index only includes about 200 Terabytes of data, which means Google has indexed only 0.004% of all data on the internet. The human brain can only hold 1 to 10 terabytes of data.* So no WONDER you are feeling overwhelmed!

What are metrics?
Metrics are how to see if you're getting heard by enough people to move your business forward.

What should we measure to get our metrics?

For your website, you can use Google analytics to measure:

Uniques: This is the number of unique visitors your website has
Visits: How many times people visit your site in a given period of time
Your most popular content: What do people read a lot?
How people find you: What keywords lead people to your website

For your social media channels, it's worthwhile to measure how many followers you have, how many times your content gets spread by others, and the general tenor of comments about you, aka sentiment analysis or sentiment metrics.

Which metrics are important?

- Metrics that measure your engagement on social media channels
- Metrics that measure engagement on your website
- Metrics that measure your bottom line after your social media campaign.

Remember that data is not information.
You need to translate your data into something you can act on.

The difference between the new marketing reality and the old is that if you just PUSHED and BLASTED your message out there, then people would say it was adequate. Now you need to be thinking about how much you're engaging in relationship building and chatting with your audience, which is much trickier to measure, but which leads to more loyal customers over time.

Beginning Metrics

---

* http://www.webanalyticsworld.net/2010/11/google-indexes-only-0004-of-all-data-on.html

What *doesn't* matter:

- Website hits
- Website Kilobytes
- The number of Twitter followers you have if you don't have any engagement history with them.
- The number of Facebook LIKES you have
- Klout or Kred.**

What *DOES* matter:
On your website: Visits, Uniques, Pages, Comments, # of times things are copied off your site

On Twitter and LinkedIn: Mentions, Retweets, Conversations, # of influencers you have built relationships with, and, of course, followers.

What is the value of a Twitter follower? Well, there are calculators that can help you figure out your ROI on each Twitter follower*** or how much your Twitter account is worth****, but I think the best measure of whether you're succeeding online or not is to look at engagement over time.

Advanced Metrics

Behavioral metrics: How viewers behave on your social media sites or on your website. Do they abandon the shopping cart halfway through to buying or donating? Do they click around, get frustrated and go back to something else? There are different tools you can use to find out what your visitors are doing in real time.

Customer Mood: Measuring how people feel about your brand based on surveys and what you find in searches for your name and brand across the whole internet.

Ratios: Figuring out how many people have to come to your website, sign up for your newsletter, or follow you on various channels before they decide to buy your products or services.

**In my opinion, Klout is arbitrary and seems more like a popularity contest than an actual tool that will help you measure potential audience and sales for your business. So if someone tells you they have a high Klout score or Kred score, you don't have to be impressed.

***http://kluriganalytics.com/2010/04/15/social-media-roi-value-of-a-Twitter-follower/
http://www.adweek.com/news/technology/value-fan-social-media-360-102063

****http://tweetvalue.com/

Segmenting: Creating different sections of your website or social media strategy to talk to specific kinds of people, maybe 3-4 personas based on demographics.

Extra Credit: If you are a data nerd, check out geocoding and lead scoring. Also, if you want to get in on hashtag chats around measuring your marketing effectiveness, check out these: **#iprmeasure #measurePR**. There's also a Twitter account around this too, @iprmeasure.)

Problem: How to create a dashboard for listening and for measuring social media?

Now that you know which metrics are important, which tools should you be using to measure them?

Spreadsheets are fine in the short term, but in the long term, think about what data you want to track and how to create a dashboard around it, and how to apply the data to your actions. Link your analysis to your decisions.

Starting out

For the first 18 months when you start a social media presence, measure Frequency, Reach, and Yield.

- **Frequency** means how many times your brand or business is mentioned in social media channels.
- **Reach** means how many people potentially saw your brand mentioned.
- **Yield** means how this is overlaid on your business objectives, which can be called conversions, like getting people to sign up for your e-newsletter all the way up to buying your products.

Figure out where you are

When you start measuring your social media presence, establish a baseline. How many times were you getting mentioned before you started? How many people were coming to your website before you began? And what were your sales or donations like? How about your e-newsletter signups?

Figure out how often to get on social media channels.

Get your activity on a timeline. Did you tweet 10x a day, and how did that affect your website traffic? Did you do 3 blog posts this week? How did THAT affect sales? You can start with a spreadsheet, and some tools will make this even easier to measure, such as TwitSprout or SproutSocial. Look for patterns in when you use social media and if this impacts anything that people do.

Watch your metrics and make note of them.
You can do this manually, OR you can use a service or three to do this. Measure what people do right before they buy from you or donate to you. Do they take a webinar? Do they sign up for your e-newsletter?

Solutions for Tracking Your Progress:

Website Metrics

- **http://SEOBook.com** What is SEOBook? It's a free tool from HubSpot that sits inside your browser that shows you how many incoming links a website has, how old a website is, and other information. The reason this will be useful to you is because you can count how many new incoming links you have, month by month, as more and more people discover you.

- **http://Alexa.com** What is Alexa? A free tool that allows you to see demographics on who comes to your website, (such as are they male or female, do they surf from work or home, do they have children, have they completed college or grad school) how long they stay there, how many pages they look at, on average, and your international and national ranking in search engines.

- Your Website Stats. How do you track your website stats? You can use Google Analytics, or another tool. You want to track
  Uniques: Number of unique visitors to your website
  Visits: Number of visits per day and per month and
  Pages: Number of pages people view on your site per month

Twitter Metrics that Matter

Who gets to your website from Twitter? Twitter does not show you the traffic that comes to you from Twitter, but you CAN figure this out a few different ways.

- You can have a custom landing page for Twitter visitors on your website, and track the visits to that page.

- You can also track when you do Twitter outreach, and how traffic to your website rises on those days.

Other Twitter Metrics that Matter

- **Mentions:** When you have a Twitter account, you'll notice how people will mention you, with an "@" symbol.

- **Number of Followers:** This is one way to track your progress, but it isn't the most important one. Still, the more targeted followers you have, the bigger your broadcast network is. Do NOT buy followers. This will only backfire.

- **Retweets:** You can REACH farther when people retweet you. If someone with 20,000 followers retweets you for example, then suddenly, you have 20,000 more potential eyeballs looking at your blog, your Twitter account, than before. You might have more followers and more website traffic because of that, which eventually translates into more sales.

Twitter Metrics Tools:

- **http://Twitalyzer.com:** It helps you find your most powerful followers and retweeters. It helps you see how your influence is expanding or contracting.

- **http://TweetReach.com**: When you use Tweetreach, this tool will allow you to see the maximum number of potential people that are looking at your tweets for a given week, based on mentions and retweets as well as the size of your own audience.

- **http://Tweet.grader.com :** This is from Hubspot, this will show you how fast your account grows, if you are gaining or losing followers, and fun charts.

- **http://TwitSprout.com:** Will show you how fast your Twitter account is growing, the ratio of followers to following that you have, and how fast or slow you're losing or gaining followers over the course of a week.

LinkedIn Metrics That Matter

- How many times you've appeared in search results, and
- How many times people have looked at your profile.

- The number of best answers you have,
- The number of groups you're active in, and
- The number of people who come to your website from LinkedIn
- The number of active people in your LinkedIn Group
- The number of crowd-sourced blog posts you create from LinkedIn Answers
- The number of people answering your surveys in your LinkedIn Group
- The number of people commenting or "liking" your updates
- The number of people endorsing your skills
- The number of people giving testimonials about your services on your LinkedIn Business Services page

What if I need something that measures LinkedIn and Twitter?

- **Http://SproutSocial.com** will give you many different metrics, including gender & age metrics, who is retweeting you, and how much "influence" you have.

- **http://Peoplebrowsr.com** will measure not just numbers of mentions you have, (shown on the next page) But this site will also show you sentiment metrics over time. This means what people feel about your brand. There is a sample of sentiment metrics of a campaign I did in September, 2011, for Fundraising Rockstars.

- **You can look at Ken Burbary's wiki** for new tools. http://wiki.kenburbary.com/social-media-monitoring-wiki I love this wiki because it lists tools, but you can also sort them by free versus paid, and by what they monitor. Warning: He doesn't always delete inactive websites.

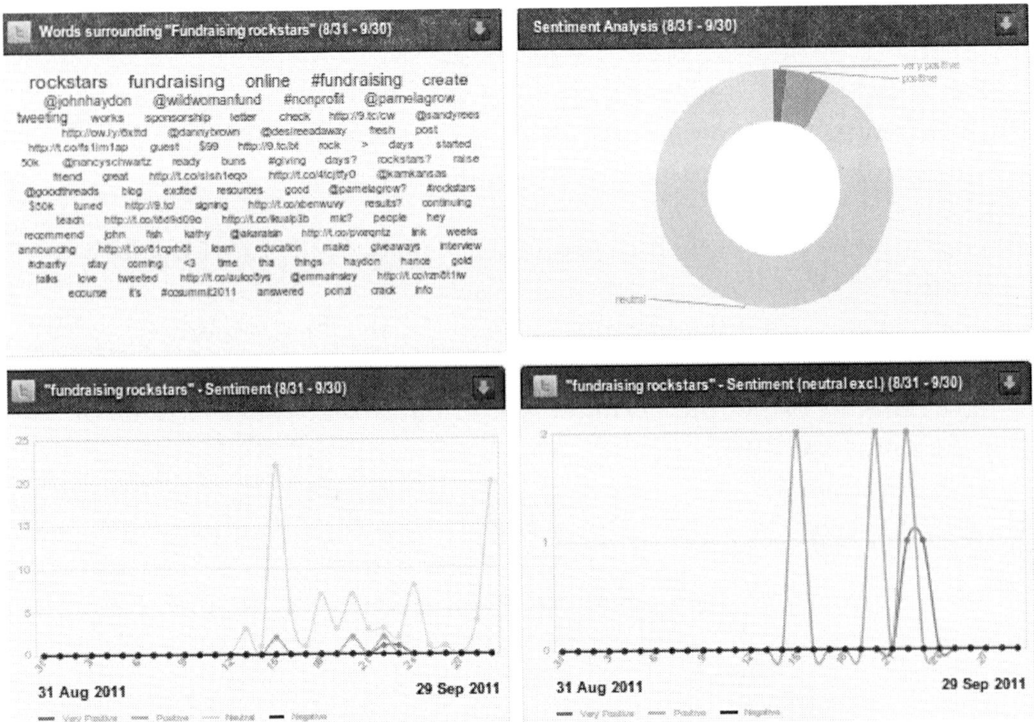

Example of PeopleBrowsr.com sentiment metrics

Sales

Ultimately, this is the true ROI and bottom line that you're looking for in all of your social media endeavors. But as any good business leader will tell you, it takes time to build up business relationships. You have to build social capital before you take your money out of the social capital bank.

Since people use email more than ANYTHING else, it's important to cultivate your email lists to affect your bottom line. Whatever else you measure with your social media dashboards, you need to measure how many people are signing up for your e-newsletter and make that number grow as fast as you can. All of your efforts, whether it's your Twitter stream, Facebook page, LinkedIn group, or YouTube channel, should encourage people to come back to your website and sign up for your e-newsletter. This is the best way to get people to buy.

Now that you know how to measure and monitor how many mentions you're getting, and how much traffic you're getting, you also need to pay attention to what people say and what their mood is when they interact with you. You need a listening dashboard to help you promptly deliver customer service.

Bad reviews cost you business! You need a listening dashboard.

"A negative remark on social media equates to a loss of 30 potential customers—but this also means that a positive review may help you gain 30 new customers.[****]*"*

Review sites like Yelp or Amazon or Angie's List can make or break a product or destination. Yelp helps local restaurants and other businesses get verified by people who want to make sure they're going to a good place. Yelp has been accused of extorting advertising money from businesses in exchange for highlighting the good reviews[*****]. Amazon sells just about everything (though they have been accused of burying the bad reviews too[******]) Angie's List helps people find good services[*******], including hotels and motels.

Imagine if someone said on Angie's List that your hotel had bedbugs. In that case, if this came up when people searched for hotels in your region, they probably would pass you by. You could be losing millions in revenue every year because of this bad review.

So when you're thinking of keywords, you must be thorough, use keyword search not just for your name, but also for your brand, product or service name and your corporate leadership.

Think about your business, and think of a phrase specific to what your customers need? For example, do they need the cleanest hotel in Miami or an international all-night youth hostel Berlin?

How to create a listening dashboard?

Just how can you monitor what people are saying about you?

****http://www.penn-olson.com/2010/04/20/4-disturbing-social-media-statistics-for-businesses/

*****http://pixsym.com/blog/reputation-management/yelp-extortion-the-lawsuits-dismissed-are-they-back-at-it-in-2012

******http://paidcontent.org/2011/06/24/419-what-shoppers-dont-realize-about-amazons-reviews/

*******http://www.angieslist.com/

Well, you COULD spend money on: Curata, Equentia, Lingospot, Brandwatch, Samepoint, GetSatisfaction, Radian6, Eloqua, etc, and if you're part of a big corporation and have a big budget to buy that software, then check out which software solution you'd like.

OR

If you can't afford to spend a lot, you could get a free account with Netvibes.com and DIY!

Start to listen. Here's how to set up a listening dashboard for your organization or company.

1. Get a http://netvibes.com account and learn how to add feeds (just read the end of the previous chapter if you skipped it).
2. Set up Google or socialmention alerts for your name, your business or organization's name, and for keywords related to your industry. If you're an orchestra, it would be "orchestra" and your city and state for example.
3. Research where people are talking. Look at http://alltop.com http://technorati.com and do a Google search of blogs
4. Check out other ways to listen. There are so many more, so I encourage you to go and see which ones are right for you.

Where do you go from here?

From here, you should go play with metrics tools, and try to find quick ways to get the data you need. If your boss likes charts and graphs, make sure the tool you choose has these in it. If your boss likes quotes from customers or users, make sure that you incorporate customer mood via quotes into your analysis. For the first 18 months, do not overlay your social media metrics onto the bottom line. After 18 months, you can start to do so. You can also overlay your metrics on top of mentions in offline media, for another way to show that the profile of your company is rising.

Must Know

- It's key to monitor what people are saying about you online. You can pay for services to do it for you, or you can do it yourself.
- Your boss wants to see hard sales numbers. In the beginning, you can show you're increasing the volume of the conversation about you, reminding people that you exist, and dealing with customer

service through social media.
- If your boss wants you to focus on email marketing to get more sales, make sure you have a budget to buy lists or focus with an email marketing team at your e-newsletter provider.

Must Do

- Create a spreadsheet with influencers in the niche and track how much you're interacting with them, and figure out what you want from them. Do you want them to feature you on their blog? List you in their resources section? Tell their list about you? Live blog your conference? Do a co-branded webinar with you? Whatever it is, have a spreadsheet to track it.
- Update your social media channels at least once a week with one sales message about your brand, but spend the rest of the time just chatting with people, whether though a Twitter chat, or mentioning and complimenting influencers.
- Always have a reason for people to sign up for your e-newsletter list. What do they get? A discount on something? An ebook? A video? Give them new reasons as often as you like.
- *Fill out the Metrics worksheets in the back of the book.*

End of Chapter Questions:

What is important to measure for website stats?
What is unimportant to measure?
Why should you NOT buy followers?

Chapter 8: Finding Time To Do It All in 15 Minutes a Day

What is it? It's time to get your processes in place so you don't drive yourself crazy.	**When to do it** Five Days a week
What you'll need Automation tools such as: Hootsuite, Tweetdeck, Netvibes, etc.	**What to do:** Set up different sentences from your blog post into tweets, send out in the morning with customized shortened URLs. Use Netvibes to keep track of industry happenings and comment on three to ten blogs per night. Participate in Twitter chats. Post a blog post. *Fill out the 30 Day Plan for Getting Your Website from Zero to Sixty in the back of the book.*

You can be successful too! Now you know why it's so important to be found online, and how you can start to build relationships with potential donors or potential buyers.

Here's how you can start building a community of buyers or donors online, in 15 minutes a day.

For the first day, make sure you do these three things. (Setting up your website)

1. Go to Joker.com. Search for a domain name that you like.
2. Buy the domain for 2 years. (At the time of this writing, October 2012, this costs around $20 US.)

3. Get hosting with Dreamhost.com or http://Arieslabs.com.
4. Go to http://freewpthemes.net to find out which Wordpress theme you'd like for your site. If you have a little money, check out the Headway theme or the SimplePress themes.
5. Get your Wordpress theme installed and your website set up.

Next day. (Social Networks)

6. Create a LinkedIn account
7. Create a Twitter account
8. Create a Hootsuite account. Link your LinkedIn and Twitter accounts.
9. Set up tweets inside Hootsuite. 2 will do for now. Set them to go live one day from now.
10. Get more followers fast by signing up for TweetBig.com's free trial. Start following your favorite people in your niche on there, and type in keywords for your niche. You will be able to follow people automatically with TweetBig.

Third day. (Your first blog post)

11. Find a fun video about your niche on YouTube or another video site.
12. Copy the embed code, and put it into a post in your Wordpress blog.
13. Write what you think of the video below the video.
14. Make sure to put your keywords in the post as tags, in the subject, and in the body of the post. For example, if you work in the food and beverage industry, your keywords might be: “Barista training” “coffee making techniques” “fabulous foam art” etc.

Create a few more blog posts. You can take things you have learned from your experiences at work in your niche and write about them. Or if you're exploring a new niche, write about your learning process.

Fourth through Ninth Days: Continue creating blog posts, tweeting, and talking to people online.

Once you have this rhythm down, add this last step.

Tenth Day. (Commenting)

10. Here is where things get fun. Look for blogs in your niche talking about what you've written your post about. Look for recent articles, not old articles. Comment below the post about your

experience or research in the field, and then ask for their comments on your post. Comment on three to ten blogs per night.

If you repeat this process for three months, your traffic will rise exponentially. JUST WATCH.

Once you stop reading this book, don't just lay it down. Get online.

Find my Twitter account, Http://Twitter.com/wildwomanfund Follow me & say hi!

Sign up for my free e-newsletter where I'll keep you up to date on all of the latest social media tips and tricks! Http://wildsocialmedia.com.

I love the fact you're reading this, but now it's time to work! If you've put off your worksheets, do them now.

If you've put off buying your name domain, go to http://joker.com and do it now.

If you've put off everything because you want someone to do it for you, give me a call. If I can do it, I will, and if I can't, I will connect you, personally, with people to do it for you.

Chapter 9: Staying Private Online

One of the first questions people ask me when they start to have their own website or to get out there on social media is, what about my privacy? What are the issues with being out there online?

You have total control over what you share on your own blog, on Twitter and on LinkedIn. If you want to be private, you should simply write about business or work topics that are not personal.

But what about privacy and tracking in other ways? If you surf the internet at all, your privacy is already compromised, and you may not even be aware of it.

The company that controls the data controls the customer.

Amazon.com has shown us this as we have seen the slow erosion of the publishing industry. Book publishers used to know who bought their books. Now most people buy books on Amazon.com. Amazon does not share this information with anyone, but only uses it internally to get people browsing their website to potentially buy more by offering "suggested" books.*

If you don't believe me that you're being tracked, install Collusion as a Firefox add-on. Here's the link: http://mozilla.org/collusion. This site builds a picture of how websites are tracking you. When you activate this plugin and then start to visit your favorite websites, watch what happens in Collusion. It will start to build a picture of how these websites track you, and how the ad networks talk to each other. It's kind of scary. It starts to look like a giant spiderweb. As of October 2012, Microsoft is now coming out with a new version of their browser that

*This is hurting the publishing industry, as well as self-published authors. This is why I choose not to have my books on Amazon.com. I like knowing who has bought my books. For more details: http://blog.penelopetrunk.com/2012/07/09/how-i-got-a-big-advance-from-a-big-publisher-and-self-published-anyway/

has "Do Not Track" as an option, and marketers are not happy about it.** Firefox and Opera web browsers also have the "Do Not Track" option***. So if you take your online privacy seriously, you'll want to take these next steps.

Staying Private Online Step by Step

To help keep yourself from becoming just another commodity in this increasingly compromised online environment, you need to take certain precautions. The tools I recommend in the next few steps are all free and I use them every day.

1. *Get off of free email services* like Gmail, Yahoo, and MSN. Use a service like Thunderbird instead. If you MUST have Gmail, or another free service like Yahoo, do not log in except when you're checking your email. Then log out. These services mine where you go online and scan your email to give you targeted ads both inside your email client and on other websites such as YouTube or Huffpost. If you want to get rid of ads on these networks, I'll tell you how to do that in a minute.

2. *Turn off ads.* To opt out of the advertisements on the internet, you want to install Adblock Plus for Firefox. Go to http://adblockplus.org.

3. *Turn off ads on social network platforms*, like Google+, Facebook, Gmail, Yahoo, Google, Twitter, LinkedIn, etc. How do you do that? Install Stylish Add-on for Firefox. http://addons.mozilla.org/en-US/firefox/addon/stylish Then search for and install Stylish themes that block ads on your favorite social platforms at http://userstyles.org. I suggest the Stylish themes that have been updated most recently. You can always uninstall these themes if you don't like them.

4. *Turn off ad tracking networks:* Using Adblock does not stop ad networks from tracking you, so you also need to install Ghostery for Firefox or Chrome, at http://ghostery.com.

** http://www.nytimes.com/2012/10/14/technology/do-not-track-movement-is-drawing-advertisers-fire.html?_r=1&src=rechp

***To turn on the Do Not Track in Firefox, go here for instructions: http://support.mozilla.org/en-US/kb/how-do-i-turn-do-not-track-feature

What is Ghostery? It helps you move through the web without being tracked. Once you install it, you'll be surprised at how many sites try to track various things about you. The trackers they have blocked will appear in a purple box on the right hand side of your screen. These trackers can track everything from what you click on to other websites that you have visited, and start to build a profile about you.

5. *Secure Browsing is a must:* Once you've taken these precautions, take the next step and install Https Everywhere. http://www.eff.org/https-everywhere.

   What is Https-Everywhere? You may recognize that http is the beginning of every web address. HTTP stands for Hypertext Transport Protocol. The extra S stands for Secure, so Https means that the connection is secure. That means that no one can listen in on where you're going online. Most websites don't protect you from this. When you enable Https-Everywhere, you'll be able to surf secure in the knowledge that no one else can listen in on what you're doing online.

6. *Other ways to stay private:*
   Install the Aries Cookie Block Firefox Add-On, which will prevent websites from setting cookies. This means those advertisers won't learn which websites you visited, and in what order. That's important, so you can stay private with your browsing habits online.[****] You can get this free Add-On here. http://addons.mozilla.org/en-US/firefox/addon/aries-cookie-block/

7. If you're a super private person, I would recommend turning your cellphone off whenever you can because of what happens when you turn it on. You become a walking GPS unit and stores, ad networks, and even law enforcement can track where you are. That means that stores know where you go in the mall, and if they have access to your email, phone number, or address, they will start sending you catalogues, even if you don't buy anything. If you are unwilling to have the world know about your every move, turning off your phone is a good idea. If you'd like more details

---

******Full disclosure, I am a member of the Aries Labs co-op, which created this Add-On.*

on this, go here: http://nplusonemag.com/leave-your-cellphone-at-home.

All of these methods will help keep you more private online than the vast majority of people, and will keep your data out of the advertisers' hands. Good job!

Must Know:

- Your data is the product on the internet when you use free services.
- The more advertisers can know, the more they WANT to know. They want to learn how to manipulate you.
- You have the right to privacy, and you need to fight back.

Must Do:

- Download Firefox.
- Install Adblock Plus.
- Install Ghostery.

Chapter 10: Don't drink the unicorns

Now that I've given you a pep talk about marketing your business online, let me show you the dark side. People say, Don't drink the Kool-Aid, or don't believe in the social media unicorns, and I'm here to tell you, Don't drink the unicorns!

Social Media can be a fabulous place to play, but just having a website is not enough. Having a social media presence on various platforms is not enough either.

What do you need to be successful in making money online?

1. You have to have something people want to buy.
2. You have to have a business plan.
3. You have to have a marketing plan.
4. You have to be able to articulate what makes you different from your competitors.
5. You have to be able to write very well about every aspect of the people's pain, agendas and goals.
6. You have to be consistent, every week.
7. You have to be able to create partnerships with people to help them sell your products and services.

If you don't have time to do this, or hire someone to help you do any of the above, then don't think that this book can help you overcome that.

Just being online doesn't exempt you from the traditional rules of business.

But what if some people are telling you that “you CAN make easy money online?”

Who might be telling you this?

There are so many different scammers out there* and they are kind of like a hydra, with many heads that regenerate when you cut one off. I don't really want to give them the honor of being listed here, when there are so many good people I would rather be talking about.

How can you identify a potential scam?

If you want to find out if the information product you're about to buy is worth it, go to http://SaltyDroid.info and look at who Salty Droid, a consumer advocate, lists as dubious characters.

And if the person is not there, then go to Google and type in "person's name" plus the word scam and see what comes up.

And if nothing comes up for that, put in their name and "Warrior Forum." If they are on the Warrior Forum, don't buy their product.

Also, if the person talks about "attracting" money or "the Law of Attraction" or has products from those people on their website, then you know they are untrustworthy. The law of attraction is a scam.**

No matter how many good thoughts you have, your good vibes are no substitute for a business plan and sales people.

Finally, if someone wants to give you business advice and charge you money for it, look at their business background. Do they have experience with the kind of business that you run? Are they a person who made aerobics videos and then wrote a book about relationships? If so, why are they qualified to give business advice to you?

Don't assume that Amazon.com positive reviews are real either.

I have a friend who encouraged me to buy a vitamin product on

---

* http://www.theverge.com/2012/5/10/2984893/scamworld-get-rich-quick-schemes-mutate-into-an-online-monster

** http://saltydroid.info/supporting-bob-proctor/ also http://cosmicconnie.blogspot.com/2011/05/jerry-hicks-on-chemo-abrascam-gets.html also http://saltydroid.info/shuttering-david-schirmer/ also http://www.post-abe.blogspot.ca/

Amazon.com that's supposed to make you "hyper-creative" and "concentrated" but when I looked at the other reviews that the positive reviewers had done, they looked like cut-and-paste reviews, completely disjointed and unbelievable. So I knew that the 4 positive reviews on the product were most likely fakes.

In an interview with the New York Times***, former review seller Todd Rutherford estimates that 1/3rd of all online reviews are fakes. The practice is known as "Sock Puppeting" and it really happens and Amazon is not interested in stopping it. They are interested in selling books, not making sure that reviews are true. Let's face it. The more 5 star reviews they get, the more they are likely to sell! Don't believe the positive reviews. Do your own research.

How does the "work-from-home" scam begin?

Here's one way. They start the scam by taking out a craigslist ad, and ask you to fill out a form on a website, and then you'll be conned into buying a small product, maybe $29-$97. Then you'll start getting phone calls from what are called "boiler rooms" in Utah.

These telemarketers in the boiler rooms try to find out your weaknesses, and use a fake name, keep using YOUR name a lot, and then find out how much your credit limit is, and then they try to take all of your credit limit money.

How do I know this? Because it happened to me in 2009. I was desperate and naive and gave my phone number out on a site. I started to get harassing phone calls from these boiler room jerks, and got them for weeks. I didn't give them money, but I had to cancel my debit card so they wouldn't charge it. This is just one of the ways they get your information and what they do with it. The article on The Verge (mentioned in the previous footnote) has more information on this and other scam techniques.

What about Multi Level Marketing****?

At a recent talk that I did around social media for the City of Austin, I slammed Multi-Level Marketing (MLM) pretty hard. There was

***http://www.nytimes.com/2012/08/26/business/book-reviewers-for-hire-meet-a-demand-for-online-raves.html

****Http://en.wikipedia.org/wiki/Multi-level_marketing

someone there who took offense at this. If you've ever been part of an MLM, hear me out. It is very very difficult to make money with an MLM. So much so that most people drop out.

How does an MLM scam work? You might go to a seminar that promises that "you can make money from home!" and then that seminar leader will tell you that you need to sign up under them, and then you need to get people to sign up under you, and you'll be "making money in your sleep!" What they don't tell you is that you'll have to buy their entire product line. With Mary Kay, this costs just under $2,000. That's a lot of money to shell out for something people can get on Amazon.com or their local Walgreens for a lot cheaper. That should tell you that your main competitors are far more powerful and have a huge advantage over you.

Here's a list of some of the well-known MLMs.

- Amway
- Herbalife
- Just about any "vitamin" selling scheme that has people selling under you
- Mary Kay
- Any "free real estate" or "investing" seminar

And if you want more, go to http://mlmwatch.org. When in doubt, look up the name of the MLM and the word scam on Google. For example: "Amway scam."

If you go to an MLM pitch or "seminar," before handing over your hard-won cash, ask these questions.

- Do you give refunds?
- How much do the products I have to buy cost, all together?
- What's your rating on the Better Business Bureau?
- How much did you make last year with this system?
- Can I talk with someone who signed up last year?

Don't assume that people around you in the room are not plants that are there to "prove" the system works. When Jason Jones went to a "free real estate investing" event in Chicago in 2012[*****], he found out quickly that the people doing the presentation could not even handle the most basic questions, and there were 30 plants in the audience designed to make

*****http://saltydroid.info/jessie-conners-is-my-rich-dad/

people feel like “everyone's doing it.”

So which MLMs are not scams?

<Crickets>

What did you learn?

- If it says MLM, run far away as fast as you can.
- Don't trust a 'learn how to make money from home' scheme.
- Don't trust positive online reviews.
- Thinking positive thoughts is NO SUBSTITUTE for a business plan!
- If you have to buy the product to sell it, it's a scam.

Chapter 11: Shut Your Facebook! Turning OFF

"(We) are so inundated by information, (we) have no way to sort all this stuff out — it's like being perpetually electrocuted but not realizing it."

-Larry Fagin, poetry editor, quoted in the New York Times, September 6th, 2011.

How many hours per day do you spend online?
How many minutes per day do you text?
How much time do you spend looking at a blinking screen?

Are you totally productive for all of this time, or is there some time when you're just wasting time? How do you feel when you're wasting time? Full of passion? Or full of boredom and sadness? What could you be doing instead?

So, now you've gotten here, and you have to stop, pause, and breathe. There's a lot to do. There's not a lot of time. But this doesn't mean that you need to go full-tilt into the future with guns blazing and never stop to rest.

It's totally okay to rest, and in order to keep up any kind of social media schedule, you DO need to rest.

Call it work-life balance, call it digital detox, but whatever you call it, you need to DO IT.

Working all of the time does not mean you're productive. Working from 8am to 10pm doesn't mean you've got it all together. You have to turn off. You have to let go. You will ruin your health if you don't. Take it from me. From 2000 to 2011 American productivity increased over 400%, and corporate profits have gone up 22%, but jobs have remained stagnant.*

More and more people are being asked to take on unreasonable amounts of work because the department has been downsized or management simply does not want to divert more resources into it. If this is happening to you, you MUST put on the brakes. You MUST reclaim your time and your sanity and your boundaries. No one will do it for you.

Barbara Ehrenreich wrote a book called "Dancing In the Streets" about our capacity for collective joy, and how it's built into our societies to take time for celebration, rest, and rejuvenation, as a cure for depression. Laura Barcella interviewed Barbara Ehrenreich on Alternet and Ehrenreich says:

" We are a very social species. I was reading about it for months and months, but came across this universal pattern of ecstatic rituals — it's hard to think of any society that doesn't have them. They all seem to feature these ingredients of costuming, dancing, masking, face/body painting, feasting ... techniques that people in widely different cultures have used to generate joy. Why have we got so few [ecstatic rituals] today?

In a nutshell, generalizing over many cultures and times, these sorts of activities have been suppressed by elites — according to class, race, gender — because the [rituals] came to be seen as disruptive, subversive and even dangerous. They were seen as antithetical to the social discipline that came to be expected by mass society."

Barbara Erhenreich continues:

We have never lost the capacity for collective joy. It's part of our nature. But if you look at how little we get to exercise it . . . if we compare ourselves to the French in the 14th century, with Saint's Days and this huge calendar of festivities, we just don't do it very much, if at all.

This [lack of festivities] represents a triumph of the powerful, and their idea that you have to work all the time. This is a recent [development]. Historically, peasants worked when they had to, when they had to plant

* http://motherjones.com/politics/2011/06/speed-up-american-workers-long-hours

or harvest. When they didn't have to work, they worked on having a good time — planning festivities, costumes, dance steps; great expressions of human creativity." **

How can you get more celebration into your life?

Sit down and write out what you did today and look at it. You'll surprise yourself with how much you've done, even if it's just loading the dishwasher, folding clothes, and working on your e-newsletter a bit.

Now look at your stats, and stop and celebrate the little things. Did you get more uniques this month than last month? Celebrate with a friend. Did you get a speaking gig? Do a little dance. Did you get your first 100 subscribers to your e-newsletter? Treat yourself to acupuncture. Did you connect with 3 potential partners on Twitter this week? High-five! Go to a festival. Make a little doodle. Play a musical instrument. Allow yourself to go out and make some chalk graffiti on the sidewalk. Make a list of things you like to do, and some things you'd like to try. Be silly for awhile. It returns the spontaneity and joy to your life.

How can you tell when you need a rest?

When you start to look for ways to waste time online, when you go to your favorite celebrity gossip sites, or check your stats obsessively, or your Twitter mentions obsessively, or check your email all the time, you know you're trying to waste time. You don't have to feel ashamed. You just need to stretch and step away from the computer. Get a drink of water. Do something else.

What are some ways to get yourself away from screens?

Get off of Facebook for non-business purposes.

Seriously, you don't need to see your cousin's 300 vacation pictures. Oh, plus, you're giving Facebook a license to whatever you put on there, in perpetuity. NY Times even did an article on the ridiculous size of Facebook's privacy policy***. A word to the wise boys, bigger is not better when it comes to privacy policy. Ahem.

Get clear for your goals for the day in the morning. Do three things before you check your email. Or allow yourself to

---

** http://www.alternet.org/story/50126/?page=3

***https://www.nytimes.com/2010/05/13/technology/personaltech/13basics.html

check email only after you have accomplished certain tasks.

You'll be surprised at how much gets done.

I recommend **doing a digital detox once a week.**

Just take a break from everything. No email. No phone. No TV. No Video. No social networks. No screens of any kind.

Go to a poetry conference. Read a book in your bed. Take a bike ride with friends. Make some home-cooked meals. Write a letter. Go dancing. Paint a picture. Play your instrument. Do something completely selfish for yourself.

You'll come back, refreshed, and ready to go. Tell your friends to shut their Facebooks too, and come out to play with you.

Have a certain amount of time things need to get done in. And then say, "Okay, by 4pm I am switching to making time to wind down and start to get ready to go home, or cook dinner, or do something else.

How can you keep yourself to a timetable and a task so you don't feel guilty when you go and play?

Use the Stop Wasting Time App. It is free! And it will help you set limits on time when you work and time when you play. It will pop up on your desktop to help you make the time to do something else. When you know you've got a time limit, you tend to get work done more quickly. And you can set it for 20 minutes, 1 hour, whatever you want.

It's good for PCs, and Linux based machines. Go and download this from my extra-fun resources page at http://wildsocialmedia.com/free-stuff/

Taking Breaks Makes You More Productive

Taking digital detoxes is good for the spirit. You will be happy you did. Even if you mess up and feel like you can't take a detox, just get on the wagon again the next day.

I would not say people are addicted to the internet necessarily, any more than people are addicted to watching TV or playing games on their mobile phones. I think people choose to do these activities, and they can get excessive with the choice they have. However, if you take a day away from the computer, you will come back refreshed and renewed and much more able to concentrate on your work.****

What do you put off doing when you're wasting time on the internet?

Why postpone joy?

Must Know

- Ancient cures for depression were dancing in the streets, celebrations.
- Our society is skewed towards never taking a break, and always being more and more productive. Don't fall into this trap.
- The internet can take over your life. Don't let it.

Must Do

- Take a digital detox once a week. No internet or TV.
- Turn off your digital leash, like your cellphone or your computer, at least once a day.
- Write a physical thank you note to someone who helped you this week.
- Do something physical. Do yoga, ride your bike, do a little dance. Get outside.

****Loehr, Jim., Schwartz, Tony. *The Power of Full Engagement: Managing Energy, Not Time, Is the Key to High Performance and Personal Renewal*

Chapter 12: Where next?

If you're born on or before 1980, then you probably remember a time before the internet existed. Sometimes I get nostalgic for those times, because things seem to move so much faster now, and I'm afraid we've lost something of our humanity in the rush to get to the next thing.

Being someone who remembers a time before the internet existed, I also want to look forward and imagine a time when the internet is different than it is now.

There is so much we don't know.

We know that the internet is unimaginably vast. We look to Google to help us sift through the internet. However,

> *"Eric Schmidt, the CEO of Google, the world's largest index of the internet, estimated the size of the internet at roughly 5 million terabytes of data. That's over 5 billion gigabytes of data, or 5 trillion megabytes. Schmidt further noted that in its seven years of operations, Google has indexed roughly 200 terabytes of that, or .004% of the total size.*"*

Comic copyright Randall Munroe of XKCD.

* http://www.wisegeek.com/how-big-is-the-internet.htm

This means[**] that even though we think we're staying on top of the massive amounts of information out there, we are not even riding the wave.

Since I began writing this book in January 2011, I have seen my own views about social media evolve and online services go out of business, or radically change their privacy and business models. If I had finished this book in 2011, it would have been a very different book.

How could the internet get better?

I'd like to imagine a future when the internet helps us be even smarter about searching on it, and helps us connect with not just the information we need, but with the people who can help us ask better questions.

I'd hope that there will be more democratic sharing of local useful information, not just a redistribution of mass media or a power grab by, say, scholarly journals to lock down all of their content.

Stewart Brand, a speaking at a hacker's conference in San Francisco, said "Information wants to be free.[***]" The question is, if information is free, who will pay the creators or writers of the information? If we are all downloading music and movies for free, then how will the producers of the information get paid?

Some information sharing is good, for example, children in India are now using Khan Academy videos to learn math, because they have no money for teachers or textbooks, and they are getting better grades and there is better student retention[****].

Free information can not just benefit the tech world or kids in school. It can also benefit farmers. Check out Marcin Jakubowski's Open Source Ecology, (http://opensourceecology.org/about.php) a website, nonprofit and a movement that provides plans for farmers to build their own farming equipment, using the 50 simple machines that create a civilization. This decreases the financial burden on farmers when their equipment breaks down. Other people around the USA are creating

**Check out XKCD at http://xkcd.com/192/

***Eduardo Porter, *The Price of Everything*, pg. 137

****http://india.blogs.nytimes.com/2012/10/15/lacking-teachers-and-textbooks-indias-schools-turn-to-khan-academy-to-survive these machines, including a brick machine in Austin, Texas[*****]. Of course, it helps if you're an engineer and know how to make these tools, but still, it's a unique concept that has raised a lot of money to help people. Check out their website to see what they're working on now.

Some sharing is not good. But prosecuting people for sharing music and movies does not seem to be stopping the tide. What's the alternative? Is there a way to have both free and paid information online that respects the maker in both cases? For more details on the history of file sharing, check out this fascinating chapter called "The Price of Free" by Eduardo Porter, in his book, *The Price of Everything.*

What is the future of our current social media platforms?

People used to be on Friendster and MySpace. Then they got on Facebook and Twitter and LinkedIn. Advertisers used to know just our names, our addresses, and our emails, and now they have access to tons of other information, thanks to these networks and even our own banks sharing our purchasing history. Naturally, some people got upset about how much information was out there about them, and they decided to do something about it. If you'd like to get more private online, there are some worksheets at the end of the book that will help you.

What about online shopping? People used to be on Amazon.com and Ebay all the time. Now the online shopping space is fragmenting into more interactive brand websites and places like Etsy, where talented people create a living or part-time income through what they make.

Every social network and every shopping platform has a shelf life. The trick is, nobody knows when the expiration date is.

No one knows when the social network will stop being "the place to be." For this reason, don't build your business presence on just one platform. The main platform should always be your website. Everything in your social media should be driving people back to your website. Once they get on your email list, you can then take control of the relationship.

There are some people who say places like Facebook and Twitter are getting too commercial and cluttered.

*****http://opensourceecology.org/wiki/Replication/CreationFlame

I've heard it said that when you have a free service, YOU are the product.

If you're using a free service like Facebook, Twitter, LinkedIn, or another service, they are definitely sharing your information. Because of this, some people are getting off these networks, for example, going from Twitter to another network, called http://App.net. This is a service you can pay a monthly or yearly fee to get on, but it's sort of like a stripped down version of Twitter, with just people talking on it, like Twitter used to be, or before Twitter, Usenet.

This may just be the future of the internet. Instead of networks where we are treated like commodities and relentlessly sold to, we may choose to pay nominal fees for a network free of ads and focused on high level conversations with peers.

Wouldn't that be more useful and exciting than a glorified billboard where you can also see “conversations” from friends?

What do you think? What are some of the highest uses of the internet in the future?

Chapter 13: A 30 Day Plan for Building Community - If you have no time to read the rest of the book, this chapter is for you.

What is it? A 30 day plan if you have no idea where to start and you need to get started...YESTERDAY.	**When to do it** For 30 days.
What you'll need Twitter Account LinkedIn Account Hootsuite Account Netvibes Account Blog with Wordpress List of blogs you would like to follow.	**What to do:** See detailed 30 day plan below.

Quick Cheatsheet for Wild Social Media Success!

If you want it, in a nutshell, what this book is about, here's what it is:

First you have to LISTEN.

Next, you need to PROVIDE CONTENT.

Then you have to ENGAGE in CONVERSATIONS and build relationships with influencers.

Finally, you have to GIVE PEOPLE MULTIPLE WAYS TO BUY FROM

YOU.

How to create your digital reputation and build community:

1. Research top blogs/sites/influencers in your niche.
2. Blog one to five times a week.
3. Comment on 3-10 top blogs in your niche every night.
4. Make articles on your topic on Hubpages, EzineArticles, Squidoo.
5. Follow influencers in your niche on Twitter.
6. Retweet them, mention them, get involved in the conversation.
7. Tweet your blog posts on Twitter with different sentences, and your URL shortened with http://bit.ly.
8. Respond to blog comments quickly.
9. Be the first to comment on your blog post.
10. Submit to Blog Carnivals about your niche, or create one.
11. Put as tags describing keywords for your niche on your posts and in your header.
12. Always tag and categorize your blog posts as precisely as you can.
13. Set up your mailing list opt-in form, with incentive, and auto-responder email.
14. Guest blog once a month, encourage others to visit you with a link at the bottom of the blog post.
15. If you find someone who loves your niche as much as you, invite them to guest-post or become an affiliate.
16. Create products based on your research, and partner with influencers to create an affiliate network.

In addition to lots more traffic, lots more visitors, tons more visibility, and becoming known as a resource in your field,

- You can get offers of paid speaking engagements out of the blue.
- You can start to make connections with people all over the world.
- You get new donors and new customers.
- You get people trying to tie their brand with yours because you are trusted.

(Show this next section to your boss. You can even photocopy it for them.)

Why Should We Use Social Media?

This is why. We need to go to where our customers can hear and see us, then get them to know, like and trust us.

Trust in Advertising **April 2012**

(% of global online consumers)

	Trust completely/ somewhat	Don't trust much/At all
Recommendations from people I know	92%	8%
Consumer opinions online	70%	30%
Editorial content like newspaper articles	58%	42%
Branded websites	58%	42%
Emails I signed up for	50%	50%
Ads on TV	47%	53%
Brand Sponsorships	47%	53%
Ads in magazines	47%	53%
Billboards & outdoor ads	47%	53%
Ads in newspapers	46%	54%
Ads on the radio	42%	58%
Ads before movies	41%	59%
TV show product placements	40%	60%
Ads in search engine results	40%	60%
Online video ads	36%	64%
Ads on social networks	36%	64%
Online banner ads	33%	67%
Display ads on mobile devices	33%	67%
Text ads on mobile phones	29%	71%

(from Nielsen)

Why we need an e-newsletter

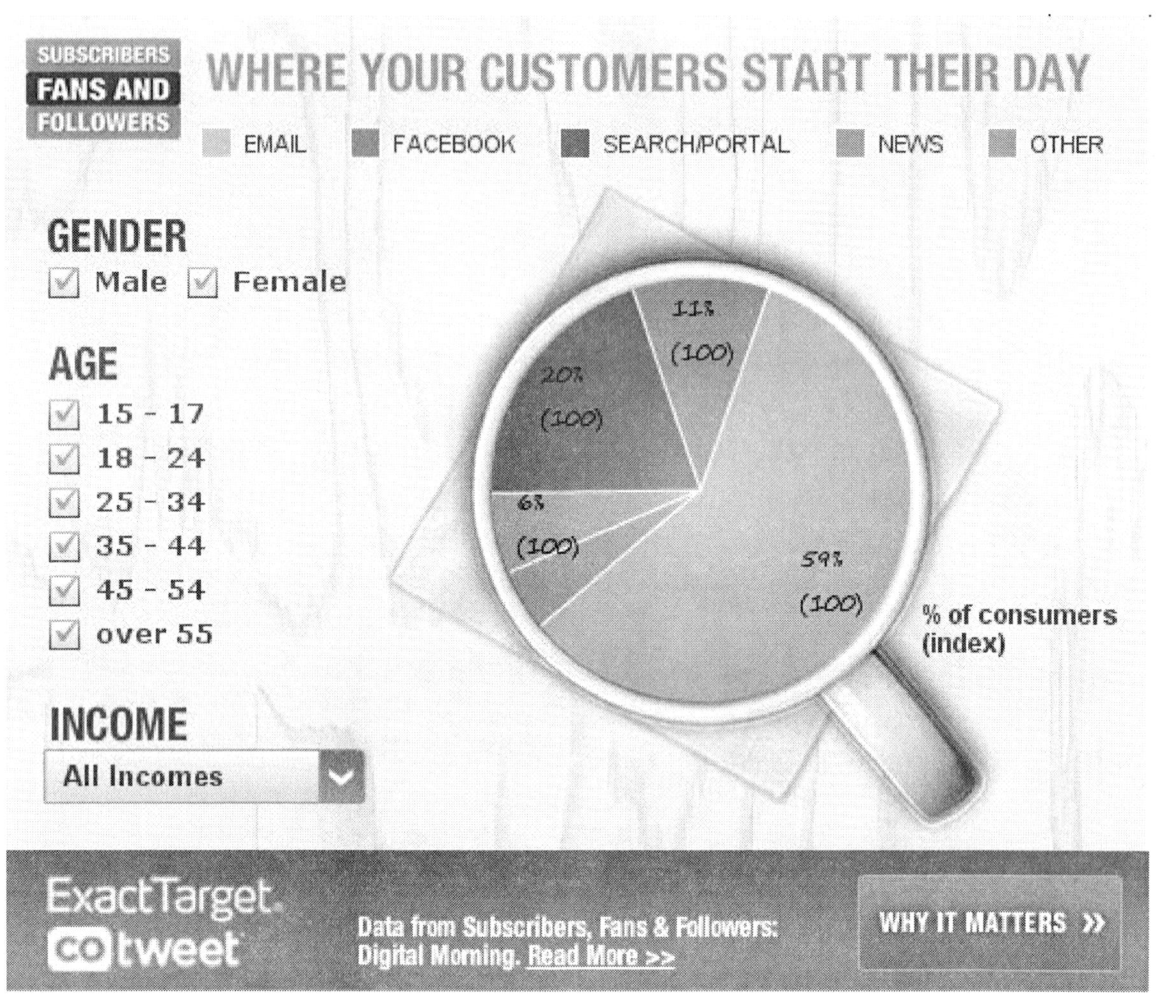

Social Media & Digital Marketing is like a WHEEL driving people back to our website to buy.

We need to choose which spokes of the wheel are going to be most powerful for our business.

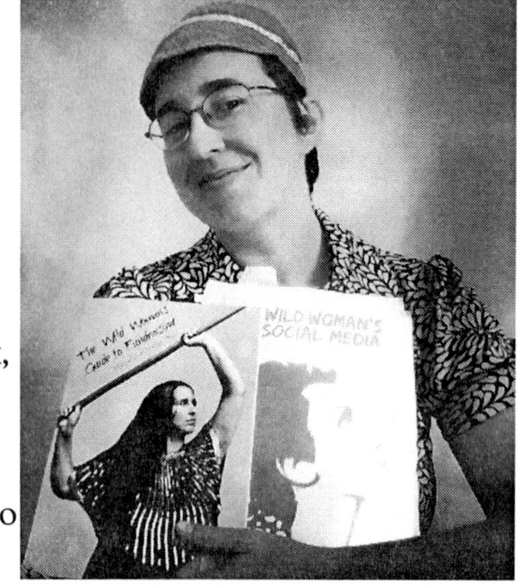

Epilogue

Even though we're at the end of the book, I still have so much to tell you!

Social media changes so fast that I want to keep you updated on the latest news, to help you stay competitive in your marketing. Sign up for my email list at http://wildsocialmedia.com and you'll get free tips on social media, the latest ways to market your business, and more!

Bring me to your town (Literally or Virtually!)

If you'd like to teach your team about social media with a webinar or a workshop on how to use social media to change donor or customer perception and behavior, or bulk book orders for your conference or group, please email mazarine@wildsocialmedia.com

Thank you so much for doing these worksheets and for reading this book! I am so proud of you!

Tell me your stories of what you've done with this book at mazarine@wildsocialmedia.com.

Tell me how I could improve the next edition at info@wildsocialmedia.com.

Selected Bibliography

On combined ways to market your business online

Evans, Dave. Social Media Marketing, an hour a day. Sybex, Wiley. 2008.

Evans, Liana. Social Media Marketing. Que. Indianapolis, IN. 2010.

Handley, Ann, Chapman, C.C. Content Rules. Wiley and Sons. Hoboken, NJ. 2011.

Harden, Leland, Heyman, Bob. Digital Engagement: Internet marketing that captures customers and builds intense brand loyalty. Amacom. New York, NY. 2009.

Hunt, Ben. Convert! Designing Web Sites to Increase Traffic and Conversion. Wiley. Indianapolis, IN. 2011.

Jantsch, John. The Referral Engine. Portfolio, Penguin Group. New York, NY. 2010.

Kaufman, Josh. The Personal MBA. Penguin Books, London, UK. 2012

Loveday, Lance, Niehaus, Sandra. Web Design for ROI: Turning Browsers into Buyers & Prospects into Leads. Pearson, 2008

Schlie, Erik. Rheinboldt, Jörg. Waesche, Niko Marcel. SimplySeven : Seven Ways to Create a Sustainable Internet Business . Palgrave Macmillan. London, UK. 2011

Scoble, Robert, Israel, Shel. Naked Conversations. Wiley. Hoboken, NJ. 2006.

Scott, David Meerman. The New Rules of Marketing & PR. Wiley.

Hoboken, NJ. 2010.

Stratten, Scott. Unmarketing. John Wiley and Sons. Hoboken, NJ. 2010.

Stelzner, Michael. Launch! John Wiley and Sons, Hoboken, NJ. 2011.

Turner, Jamie. Shah, Reshma. How to Make Money With Social Media. Pearson Education, Inc. Upper Saddle River, NJ. 2011

On Twitter

Comm, Joel. Twitter Power. How to dominate your market one tweet at a time. Wiley. Hoboken, NJ. 2009.

Israel, Shel. Twitterville. Penguin. New York, NY. 2009.

McFedries, Paul. Twitter Tips, Tricks & Tweets. Wiley & Sons. Indianapolis, IN. 2009.

Schaefer, Mark. The Tao of Twitter. Published on Amazon by Mark W. Schaefer. 2011.

On Copywriting

Bayan, Richard. Words that Sell. Contemporary Books, Chicago, IL. 1994.

Whitman, Drew Eric. Cashvertising. Career Press. Pompton Plains, NJ. 2008.

On Social Media for Nonprofits

Gibson, Andy. Courtney, Nigel. Ward. Amy Sample. Wilcox, David. Holtham, Clive. Social by Social. NESTA OpenMute, London, UK. 2009.

Kanter, Beth. Fine, Allison. The Networked Nonprofit, Jossey Bass. New York, NY. 2010.

On Networking

Baber, Anne. Waymon, Lynne. Make Your Contacts Count. Amacom. New York, NY. 2007.

Hayden, C.J. Get Clients Now! Amacom. New York, NY. 2007.

Stanley, Thomas. Selling to the Affluent. McGraw Hill Publishing. New York, NY. 1997

On ROI of social media

Blanchard, Olivier. Social Media ROI. Que. Indianapolis, Indiana. 2011.

Powell, Guy. Graves, Steven. Dimos, Jerry. ROI of Social Media. Wiley & Sons. Singapore. 2001.

Osburn. Eve Mayer. Social Media for the CEO. Emerging Media Press. 2010.

Digital Detox

Ehrenreich, Barbara. Dancing in the Streets. Metropolitan Books. New York, NY. 2006.

Loehr, Jim, Schwartz, Tony. The Power of Full Engagement: Managing Energy, Not Time, Is the Key to High Performance and Personal Renewal. The Free Press. New York, NY. 2003.

Misc.

Porter, Eduardo. The Price of Everything. Penguin. New York, NY. 2011.

Online resources:

Online advertising

The Case for In-Stream Advertising Mark Suster on November 22, 2009
http://www.bothsidesofthetable.com/2009/11/22/the-case-for-in-stream-

advertising/

Banner Blindness Jakob Nielsen on August 22, 2007 http://www.useit.com/alertbox/banner-blindness.html

The Future of Advertising will be Integrated, TechCrunch, Mark Suster on 2011 http://techcrunch.com/2011/04/29/the-future-of-advertising-will-be-integrated/

Consumer Internet Predictions, Jeremy Liew, December 11, 2010 http://lsvp.wordpress.com/2009/12/11/2010-consumer-internet-predictions/

Why Online Brand Spending will create new winners in online ad networks Jeremy Liew, July 14, 2010 http://lsvp.wordpress.com/2010/07/14/why-online-brand-spending-will-create-new-winners-in-online-ad-networks/

How to Get More People to Buy On Your Website, aka Conversion Optimization

Fogg, B.J. White Paper: *A Behavior Model for Persuasive Design* Persuasive Technology Lab , Center for the Study of Language and Information, Stanford http://captology.stanford.edu/resources

Fogg, B.J., Eckles, Dean. White Paper: *The Behavior Chain for Online Participation: How Successful Web Services Structure Persuasion* Persuasive Technology Lab , Center for the Study of Language and Information , Stanford http://captology.stanford.edu/resources

Conversion Optimization for Newsletter Signups http://www.verticalmeasures.com/conversion-optimization/increasing-conversion-rates-for-newsletter-signups

How to Manage Visual Hierarchy for Conversion: http://searchengineland.com/pop-this-how-to-manage-visual-hierarchy-for-conversion-63053

Brian Massey, The Conversion Scientist
http://Conversionscientist.com

15 guides to changing people's behavior online
http://www.behaviorwizard.org

SeeWhy On Shopping Cart Abandonment
http://seewhy.com/blog/

All posts about Conversion Optimization from Get Elastic
http://www.getelastic.com/category/conversion-optimization-marketing/

DemandBase's white-papers
http://www.demandbase.com/resources/white-papers/

The Conversionista Blog
http://www.conversionista.com/blog

How to Manage Visual Hierarchy for Conversion:
http://searchengineland.com/pop-this-how-to-manage-visual-hierarchy-for-conversion-63053

Split testing for landing page optimization:
http://sitetuners.com/free-resources/testing-tutorial/ab-split/

Gary Angel's Semphonic Blog
http://semphonic.blogs.com/semangel/

Link roundup of conversion optimization articles from UnBounce.com
http://unbounce.com/landing-pages/conversion-badass-2010/

How to Get More Traffic & Influence people

Seth Godin: How to get traffic for your blog
http://sethgodin.typepad.com/seths_blog/2006/06/how_to_get_traf.html

Choosing a topic for your blog: What NOT to write about:
http://www.seomoz.org/blog/blogging-oversaturated-market-poor-

decision

21 Tips to earn links and tweets to your blog post
http://www.seomoz.org/blog/21-tips-to-earn-links-and-tweets-to-your-blog-post

Why you don't need to mass-follow users on Twitter
http://web.archive.org/web/20100412193000/http://www.doshdosh.com/Twitter-marketing-mass-follow-users/

Ways to influence people online
http://web.archive.org/web/20100209081141/http://doshdosh.com/ways-to-influence-people-online/

How to get more members for your niche Community
http://web.archive.org/web/20100416073414/http://www.doshdosh.com/how-to-get-more-members-for-your-niche-community/

Misc. Online Resources

Here is a constantly updated wiki list of other tools you can use to monitor your online reputation, there are over 200 of them here:
http://wiki.kenburbary.com/social-meda-monitoring-wiki

A constantly updated list of social media policies
http://socialmediagovernance.com/policies.php

A good list of Content curation/News discovery tools
http://www.mindmeister.com/fr/134760952/news-discovery-tools-2012-by-robin-good

Find out fast if someone is copying your blog content:
http://copyscape.com
http://tynt.com

A couple of the hundreds of metrics tools:
http://Tweetreach.com
http://sproutsocial.com

The Wild Woman's Guide to Social Media Workbook

You've read the book. Now what? How can you apply this to your marketing NOW?

For Business Owners, Marketing Experts, Community Managers, Social Media Consultants, Fabulous Entrepreneurs who want to take action NOW:

Remember:

"You need to build Content, Context, Connection, and Community"
-John Jantsch, The Referral Engine

Let's get a shared vocabulary here. What do you have to do to get more buyers and more cash?

Online

- **Blog:** Set up a blog, updated one to three times weekly, with relevant and helpful and first hand information about your mission or your business.

- **Building email list:** Set up an e-newsletter account, add a mailing list signup form to site, give people something (e.g. PDF download) for signing up for mailing list. Then, send out weekly newsletter, with: advice, links to useful or funny articles, and invitations to things you're doing.

- **Commenting:** Finding a relevant blog post and leaving a useful and substantive reply that specifically contains a link back to your site.

- **Guest-post for other bloggers:** Create list of bloggers, retweet a couple of times, comment on their blog a couple of times, contact via email mentioning their blog and specific things you liked about it indicating that you have read their blog and care about their content and audience.

- **Contact Influencers:** Build relationships with 5-10 influencers in your niche. To do this: retweet them 5-10 times, mention them on Twitter 5 times, leave five comments on their blog. After this contact has been made, email directly and ask if they will either let you guest post or talk about the site on their Twitter account.

- **Purchase ads:** Run a few Google ads and see how they do.

- **Use Twitter:** Use Tweetbig to increase # of followers, talk with influencers, participate in hashtag chats

Offline

- **Call podcasters and ask to be a guest on their show:** Show you've done your homework, mention their previous shows and what you'd like to talk about.

- **Contact bloggers and journalists with press kit:** Develop a press kit and send to journalists. Only send to bloggers if you've built a prior relationship.

- **Attend offline meet-ups:** Find meet-ups in your city, request to be highlighted as a presenter at the meetup to talk about what you do.

Becoming an authority

All of these strategies help you not just control the first 3 pages of Google results about you, but help you become known as an authority in your field. So if people just want general advice about your field, what can they get out of your site?

- How can your site help them?

- What's something you wish you had known before becoming who you are? What mistakes do you see people making in the beginning?

- These can be seeds of a small 10-30 page ebook that you can offer for free for joining your newsletter.

Your Keywords Worksheet

What are keywords? Keywords are words that describe you, and that people often search for in reference to what you do, what you sell, or what you offer as a service. So, for example, if you're a car mechanic for Japanese cars in Des Moines, your keywords would be "car repair, Des Moines, Toyota, reliable, Honda, happy customers, Japanese automobiles, fast, fix my car, tow truck, electrical problems, alternator, affordable, honest mechanic" etc.

What are some Keywords that describe you? Write them below.

Your Competition Worksheet

Do some market research. Look around. Who else is doing what you do? What do they offer that is similar? What do they offer that is different? If you can't think of at least 3 ways that you're different from your competition, then how will you convince them to buy from you?

How are you different from your competition? Write your response below.

How are you similar in branding?	Your competitor name

How are you different?	Your competitor name

Who You Are Worksheet

We're going to figure out what makes you unique, and what you'll be selling. This is called your Unique Selling Proposition, or USP for short.

1. What are you selling now?

2. What do you enjoy doing the most/know a lot about?

3. What do (or could) you provide that no one else is providing?

4. What annoys people the most about your industry?

5. What is remarkable about you?

6. Write a Unique Selling Proposition (USP) statement

Use the following format:
I am unique and different because I provide [USP] which no one else in my field provides. No one else can or will provide this because [insert reason].

Who To Write For Worksheet

What You Need is a Persona. Who is most likely to buy your products and services? And what should you offer? To figure out what you should offer, answer these questions.

How old are they?

Income bracket?

Hobbies?

Where do they live?

Why do they come to you versus someone else?

Disposable income?

What is the person's level of education?

What are some typical job titles?

Does this persona require a specific skill set, degree, certification, or other continuing education?

How does this persona typically seek new information and keep up to date with the industry?

What events do they attend?

What do they read? Online and off? *

What are this persona's most important job responsibilities and activities?

Which ones relate most closely with your products?

---

* Some of these questions are borrowed from Jeremy Victor. http://www.b2bbloggers.com/blog/how-to-create-buyer-personas/

What are the top three – five challenges or problems for this individual in their job?

Which ones relate most closely with your products?

How does this persona measure success?

Do any of your products have the ability to help them achieve that?

How is this persona's success measured? By whom (what stakeholders)?

What's at risk for this individual in the purchasing process?

What could go wrong for them if the purchase is a failure?

What has prevented this persona from considering your products in the past?

What is the person's likely progression within their career?

What other roles have they had?

What do they aspire to become?

What Your Audience Wants Worksheet

Do you tailor content for each particular group that comes to your website? Would you have a place on your site for each kind of person who comes there? Or would you like to focus on the high yield kind of person?

This next section speaks to people who have an awareness of the problem, who may know of other solutions, but do not know about your solution yet.

Who in your experience, is the kind of person that buys your services? What problems, agendas, costs, and rewards do your clients have? And how do you help?

Problems	Agenda	Costs	Rewards	How you help
Example: Have been burned by bad <niche providers>.	Need reliable, efficient, and reasonably priced.	It's hard to find a good <niche provider>. Once they find you, they will want to keep you.	Want to get this particular thing quick, cheap, and good.	You provide what they want, when they want it, high quality.

Now it's your turn.

My Business Name:______________________________

My customer profile:______________________________

Problems	Agenda	Costs	Rewards	How you help

What To Write About Worksheet

Update your blog, 500-1000 word posts, or interviews, or videos or radio shows with KEYWORD RICH TOPICS. At least once a week.

The reason my traffic started to spike after February 2010 is because I started posting 5 days a week and commenting every night.

My best advice about writing is, Do not wait for inspiration. There is no inspiration. Only work. By the time you've got done waiting, two weeks may have passed, and you're no better at writing now than you were two weeks ago. So begin. How can you begin?

Remember Your Awareness ladder:
No awareness of problem: Level 0
Awareness of problem: Level 1
Solution to problem: Level 2
Your solution to the problem: Level 3
Benefits of your solution: Level 4
Buying your solution: Level 5

Write to levels 1-2. This is where your most likely potential customers or donors are.

What are some blog posts you could write for when people are first aware they need your product or service? What problem do they have? What agenda do they have?

What are some solutions to the problem? Who are your competitors? What do they offer?

Top Tips if You're Stuck

Write down everything you can remember about your niche.

- What are all of the things you know how to do? Write these down.
- What are things you find so fascinating that you could spend weeks on the topic?
- What are some hot button issues in your niche?

Research in the library and online.

- Go to your topic in the library. Scan tables of contents, and consider if you have things to say about these topics.
- Go to your RSS feeds and scan your blogs. What are they writing about that you would like to comment on? Turn those comments into blog posts.
- Go to your local association meeting or read a newspaper. What are they talking about or writing about? Turn their conversation into a blog post.

Find your heroes and heroines, and interview them.

- It could be a person in your niche offline or online.
- It could be a gathering together of your heroines at a conference.
- It could be an imaginary interview with a person who has passed on. Glean wisdom however you can, and help your name be associated with people who have already made it.

Possible Blog Post Topics Checklist

50 Blog Post Ideas	
Stop worrying about being wrong.	
Ask a question.	
Think about your pain.	
Do a book review.	
Think funny.	
Tweet about needing ideas.	
Mine your hobbies.	
Try a new medium.	
Do an interview.	
Take a hike.	
Have a debate.	
Write something else.	
Talk about your mistakes.	
Make a prediction.	
Review the past.	
Create a regular feature.	
Where are they now?	
Change your view.	
Eavesdrop.	
Take a bath.	
Take a poll.	
Read trade publications.	
Skim national newspapers and magazine stories.	
Ask yourself, "What's missing?" or "What will happen next?"	
Read small publications.	
Riff on a popular post.	
Read your social-media group's questions.	
Talk to a friend.	
Tackle a controversy.	
Join a blogger's group.	
Scan industry conference schedules.	
Get a critique.	
Hold a contest.	
Keep a journal.	
Free associate.	
Do a mind map.	
Do a product review.	

Run your analytics.	
Read your comments.	
Read your competitors.	
Read your competitors' comments.	
Hit an industry networking event.	
Attend a local community event.	
Google alerts. Set an alert with a few industry keywords.	
Review your greatest hits.	
Write a sequel.	
Participate in a blog carnival.	
Recruit a guest.	
Take an entire day off — every week.*	

Go back to your ideal reader, or people who have bought from you in the past.

What information do THEY need to know?

How do THEY like to think of themselves?

What problem of theirs can you help solve?

What questions can you help answer?

What are typical confusions people have in your field?

I hope this is enough to get you started!

Interviews Worksheet

Coming up with content, the sneaky way:

What do you wish you knew more about, in your industry?

Who does know more about it?

People you can guest post for: Heroes or peers (and have access to their audience!)

People you can ask for guest posts or interviews

PS. You can totally ask me for a guest post or interview if you want to! :)

30 Day Checklist for Getting your Web Presence from Zero to 60

I did it!	What to do
	DAY 1: Research a good domain name with Wordoid.com or http://Joker.com, related to who you are or what you do. Your name domain is good to get.
	DAY 2: Register your domain name with Joker.com, and buy hosting with Dreamhost or http://Arieslabs.com.
	DAY 3: Pick a Wordpress theme, if you want a free one, go to http://freewpthemes.net, and hire a graphic designer to modify it for you, and a web developer to put it on your domain. If you want a paid theme, I like the Headway theme, Simplepress is also good.
	DAY 4: Research top keywords and phrases people generally search for in your niche via Bing, Yahoo, http://GoogleKeywordTool.com, and other search engines.
	DAY 5: Add the keywords you found to your theme's style.css page.
	DAY 6: Download your plugins (list of best plugins included in worksheets) and install Google Analytics with Google Webmaster Tools.
	DAY 7: Create 10-20 blog posts about your niche, decide how often you will post them.
	DAY 8: Use the WP calendar plugin to space these posts out over two months.
	DAY 9: Add your Twitter widget to the sidebar of your blog by going to http://TwitterCounter.com.
	DAY 10: Create a free give-away report about your niche, could be ten pages long, doesn't have to be complicated, just clear and useful.

I did it!	What to do
	DAY 11: Create a small picture of this freebie and some text for your e-newsletter signup widget.
	DAY 12: Sign up for an e-newsletter service, such as MailChimp or Aweber. Take some time to get to know the tool. Create a widget for your blog with the small picture of the free thing they get for signing up.
	DAY 13: Create a page where people can download their freebie. Add your e-newsletter signup widget to the sidebar of your blog.
	DAY 14: Sign up for http://Netvibes.com
	DAY 15: Research blogs in your niche with http://alltop.com and with Google, and other places that have listings of resources in your niche. Look for someone with engaging writing, with useful advice. ALSO
	DAY 16: Install http://SEOBook.com toolbar so that you can look at how many incoming links each site that you visit has, and work on commenting on sites with the most incoming links.
	DAY 17: Add the RSS feeds of those blogs in Netvibes
	DAY 18: Start commenting on three to ten blogs per night with relevant links back to your blog.
	DAY 19: When you have enough relevant articles, link back to your relevant article at the end of your comment, and ask people to continue the conversation there.
	DAY 20: Ping your website with http://pingomatic.com
	DAY 21: Write a press release about your new website and submit to http://prlog.org, http://prfire.cu.uk, http://pitchengine.com, http://fngpr.com
	DAY 22: Create a video and post it on your blog.
	DAY 23: Submit the video to YouTube, Vimeo, Blip.tv, TubeMogul.com.
	DAY 24: Create a podcast about your niche, and use the Blubry Powerpress Plugin to automatically upload

I did it!	What to do
	this to iTunes.
	DAY 25: Interview someone in your niche, and create an audio or video file out of this.
	DAY 26: Sign up on various social bookmarking sites via http://onlywire.com and http://socialposter.com and post your posts there.
	DAY 27: Submit your posts to a blog carnival or create your own.
	DAY 28: Metrics: Track your stats with Google Analytics and see how far you've come. Look at visits, uniques and pages.
	DAY 29: Install http://Alexa.com link on your site to keep track of your worldwide ranking.
	DAY 30: Watch your subscribers rise, engage with them and email them personally, asking them how you can help them.

How do you manage your blog workflow? Where do you go from here?

After you fill out your 30 day checklist for starting your blog, here's how it works day to day.

You create between one to five blog posts per week, and they can be about anything that your target audience cares about. Put them out there with Hootsuite onto your various social networks.

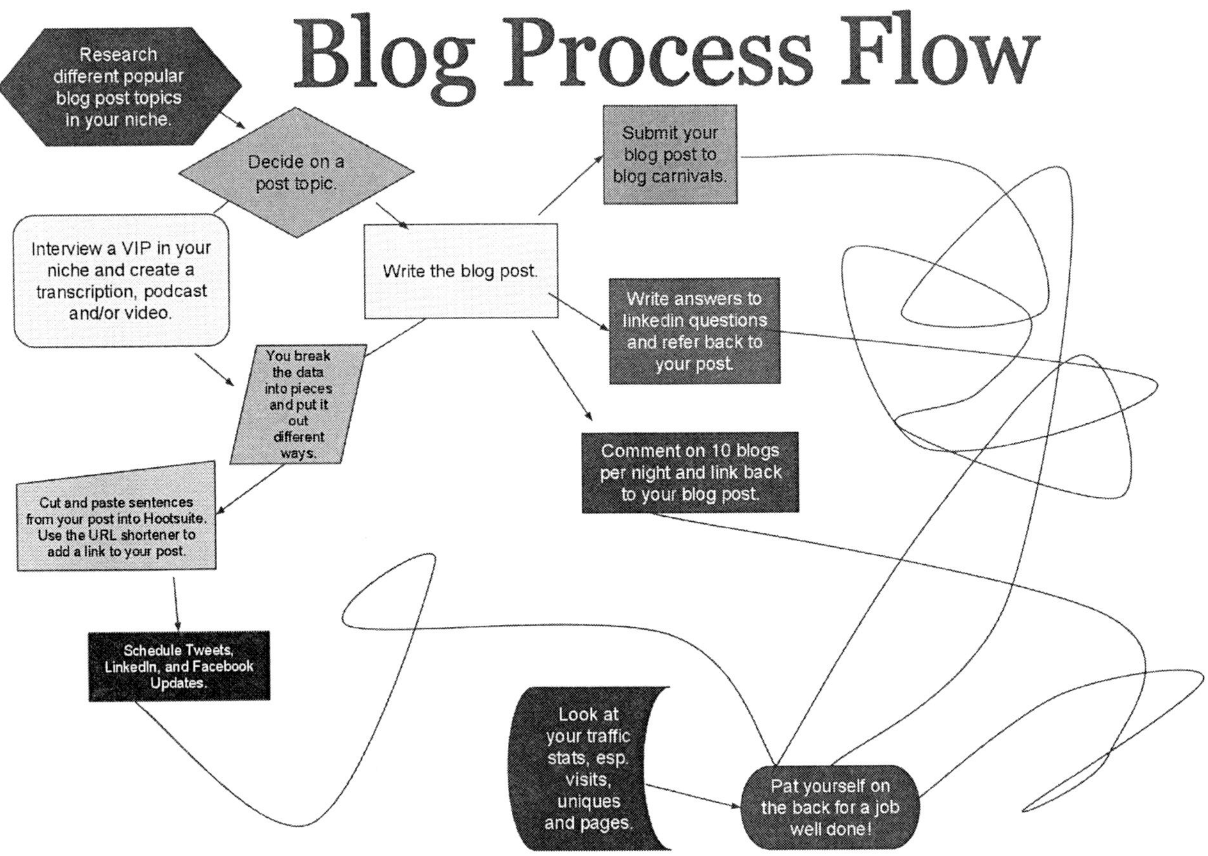
Blog Process Flow
Research different popular blog post topics in your niche.
Decide on a post topic.
Interview a VIP in your niche and create a transcription, podcast and/or video.
Write the blog post.
Submit your blog post to blog carnivals.
Write answers to linkedin questions and refer back to your post.
Comment on 10 blogs per night and link back to your blog post.
You break the data into pieces and put it out different ways.
Cut and paste sentences from your post into Hootsuite. Use the URL shortener to add a link to your post.
Schedule Tweets, LinkedIn, and Facebook Updates.
Look at your traffic stats, esp. visits, uniques and pages.
Pat yourself on the back for a job well done!

Essential Wordpress Plugins Checklist

Plugin Name	What it does	Got it?
Anti-Captcha	Anti-Captcha is a transparent captcha solution which does not require any end-user interaction.	
cbnet Ping Optimizer	Saves your Wordpress blog from getting tagged as ping spammer.	
Cool Ryan Easy Popups	Add Descriptive Popups to entice your readers with messages, opt-ins, and more!	
Google XML Sitemaps	This plugin will generate a special XML sitemap which will help search engines like Google, Yahoo, Bing and Ask.com to better index your blog.	
Growmap Anti Spambot Plugin	Very simple plugin that adds a client side generated checkbox to the comment form requesting that the user clicks it to prove they are not a spammer.	
HeadSpace2	Meta-data manager on steroids, allowing complete control over all SEO needs such as keywords/tags, titles, description, stylesheets, and many many other goodies.	
Network Publisher	Automatically publish your blog posts to multiple Social Networks including Twitter, Facebook Profile, Facebook Pages, LinkedIn, MySpace, Yammer, Yahoo, Identi.ca, and more.	
P3 Plugin Performance Profiler	Helps you figure out why your site is running slow, which plugins are causing slowness & should be deactivated.	
Page Links To	Allows you to point Wordpress pages or posts to a URL of your choosing. Good for setting up navigational links to non-WP sections of your site or to off-site resources.	
Page Theme	Per-page, per-post theme selection. Works with both SEO and non-SEO permalinks.	
SEO Slugs	Removes common words like 'a', 'the', 'in' from post slugs to improve SEO.	

SEO Title Tag	Search engine optimize your blog's title tags. Create a customized title tag for any post, static page, category page or any URL	
Sweet Captcha	This plugin makes people put an object from the left hand side on the picture on the right hand side. For example, "Give the piggy his cigar." It's more fun and can't yet be gamed by robots trying to comment spam your blog.	
Wordpress Mobile Pack	The Wordpress Mobile Pack is a complete toolkit to help mobilize your Wordpress site and blog. It includes a mobile switcher, widgets and content adaptation for mobile device characteristics.	
WP-Optimize	This plugin helps you to keep your database clean by removing post revisions and spams in a blaze. allows you to rename your admin name also.	
WP Hide Pages	Enables you to hide pages from Wordpress menus, blog searches and search engines.	
Yoast Breadcrumbs	Outputs a fully customizable breadcrumb path.	

What are some other plugins that you like? Feel free to make a note of them here, and email me to put them in the next edition of the book, at info@wildsocialmedia.com.

30 Day Plan for Dominating LinkedIn Checklist

I did it!	What to do
	DAY 1: Create your profile.
	DAY 2: Add people from your email address book.
	DAY 3: Once you are on there, find people that you know, search for previous companies that you've worked at, and invite them to connect with you.
	DAY 4: Ask your current business associates, whether coworkers or clients or bosses, to give you testimonials on LinkedIn.
	DAY 5: Write a summary of your talents and what you're looking for.
	DAY 6: When filling out your profile, You can put in your birthday and the dates you went to school, but I wouldn't. I mean, come on. Make it a LITTLE harder for scammers to impersonate you, huh?
	DAY 7: Add the jobs you feel are relevant to what you're looking for right now.
	DAY 8: Add the section where you fill in your skills, and try to brag a little bit.
	DAY 9: Search for groups related to your field. HR? Nonprofits? Sports Marketing? Accounting? Writing? Art therapy? Whatever it is, you can find a group for it, and most likely you'll find 20 groups related to it.
	DAY 10: You can also search for groups related to who you are. Are you a female entrepreneur? Are you an alumni of some college? If you were a member of a fraternity or sorority, they might be on here too! Are you a former employee of a big corporation? Are you an Japanese-American dentist? You could find a group just for you. Check out your affinity groups. If it looks like it doesn't have any activity, don't join.
	DAY 11: Now that you're in some groups, you might want to take a look around and see who are the top

I did it!	What to do
	people in your field on LinkedIn, and see which groups they belong to. If you'd like to connect to them, see if you can join a group they belong to. You'll be able to email them if you are a member of the same group.
	DAY 12: Look at companies you want to connect with. Can you "follow" them on LinkedIn? That might help you get your foot in the door for getting hired or doing business with them.
	DAY 13: Look at the questions section of LinkedIn. What fields should you look in? Corporate management? Writing and editing? Philanthropy? Do some keyword searches for your categories that you've got expertise in. Are there any questions there you feel qualified to answer?
	DAY 14: Answering your first question: Read over what other people said. Did they say what you would have said? How can you give a more complete or satisfying answer than they did? If you can't, move onto the next question. If you can, make sure to link back to your website where you have more resources about the question. And refer people who you think would know the answer to the question if you don't know. Also, write a little LinkedIn note to the person when you've answered the question. That will encourage them to look at what you did and rate your answer higher.
	DAY 15: Go back and look at who responded to your question, or if there are other questions you could answer. The more questions you answer, the more people will look at your profile.
	DAY 16: Add some books you're reading to your reading list. Add some business related books. So if you're always looking to learn about your industry, for example, lean manufacturing, put some of the books you've read on that there. Keep track of what you read, even if it's just in the bookstore. You can always mark a book that you WANT to read, even if you haven't read it yet.
	DAY 17: Create a Slideshare account and upload some

I did it!	What to do
	slideshows. Now you can add some slideshows that you've done to LinkedIn. Just select the Slideshare widget.
	DAY 18: If you are looking for work, or simply want to show off your achievements, it pays to make a custom slideshow with your achievements highlighted in it. Whether it's sales metrics or number of patients seen per week, find a way to quantify your achievements. If you have pictures, so much the better!
	DAY 19: Now it's time to start reaching out more. Who could YOU give recommendations to? Think about it. Start to connect with them on LinkedIn, and give them meaningful recommendations.
	DAY 20: Look at networking events in your town. Sometimes they are only announced on LinkedIn. Is your local chamber of commerce on LinkedIn? What about another local networking group? See if you can see when the next meetings are, and meet people there.
	DAY 21: Once you're home from the meeting, ask to connect with people that you met there on LinkedIn. Try to connect them with someone that you know who might be able to help them with a problem that they have.
	DAY 22: Look at your profile. How many different industries could you be listed under? Is it SO unfair that you can only be listed in one? Well, hold your horses Amigo. What you can do is simple. Put yourself simultaneously in multiple industries. It is going to look like you put the same job in 5 times, but you are increasing exponentially your chances of being found.
	DAY 23: Do you have a professional headshot or a picture of you in business attire? Put it up on your LinkedIn profile. People like to see the person that they're talking with. If you don't know any photographers, ask a friend to take a picture of you outside in a nice button-down shirt. Make sure the sun is not behind you or shining in your eyes. Outdoor light is generally the best for a nice-looking headshot. Unless

I did it!	What to do
	you're in the middle of a storm. Then you should probably reschedule.
	DAY 24: Look at people in your stream who are talking, and comment or respond to what they're posting about.
	DAY 25: Go back to your groups. By now, you've got a website or blog that you have posted relevant articles to. So can you put a link to your post here? YES! You can!
	DAY 26: Do you want to start a group for people like you? New entrepreneurs? Support group of some kind? Networking group with speakers? Whichever this is, see if you can put this in one of your local groups. You will get a LOT more people involved quickly this way. For example, I put the word out on local groups about a career fair on LinkedIn, and went from 500 people to 1500 people in one year at this career fair. It works.
	DAY 27: Look at the people you're now connected to. You're rocking and rolling now! Who do they know who you would like to connect with? Someone at a corporation you want to connect with for job prospects, or for sales or sponsorship prospects? Start to get strategic with your asks. Give people a REASON to connect with you. Don't just say, "I'd like to connect with you on LinkedIn." Say, "Hey, we both like crochet, and also, I see we're both in the same group! I'd love to learn more about you, and how we can collaborate!" Or something like that.
	DAY 28: Use meetup to increase your LinkedIn contacts. Go to meetup.com and look for meetups related to your field. Once you're at the meetup, start to get a sense of people there. Go a few times, and then ask people to connect with you on LinkedIn.
	DAY 29: Make your LinkedIn profile custom URL, and put it on your business card. This way, when you hand it out at networking events, you can make it EVEN EASIER for people to connect with you.
	DAY 30: By now you've seen some people who have

I did it!	What to do
	over 500 connections and seem to connect to just about EVERYBODY. And I would counsel you against doing that. You don't need to connect to EVERYBODY. Just connect with people that you WANT to connect with. Make a policy and stick to it. Pat yourself on the back for a job well done!

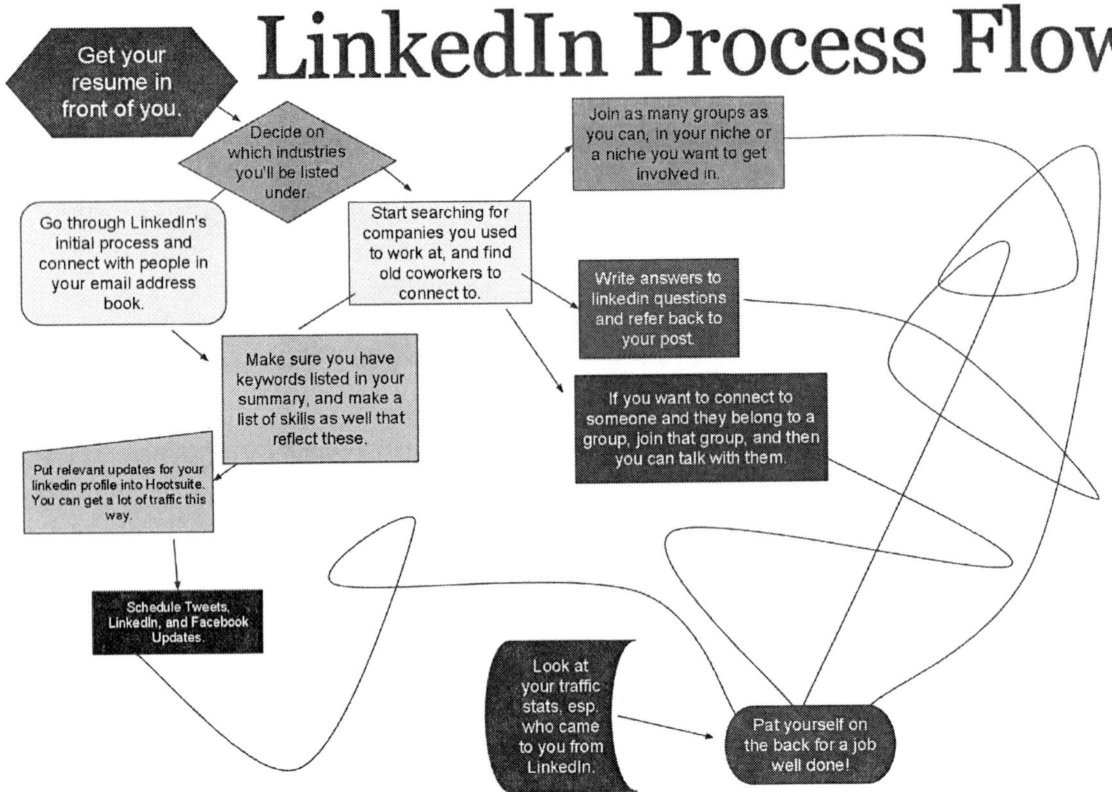

30 Day Plan for Dominating Twitter Checklist

I did it!	What to do
	DAY 1: Pick a Twitter handle that reflects your unique brand online.
	DAY 2: Search for your friends or colleagues or heroes or heroines on Twitter and follow them. If you haven't already done this, sign up for Hootsuite and link your Twitter account.
	DAY 3: Do a keyword search on Twitter for words that are common in your niche. For example, if you are a craft brewer, search for the word "beer," of course, but also "craft brewing" "biere" "bier" "cervisa" "stout" "IPA" "keg" you get the picture.
	DAY 4: Start to follow people who use these words too.
	DAY 5: If this sounds too tedious, sign up for TweetBig's free 7 day trial, and allow Tweetbig to find and follow these people for you. You still have to check off that you want to follow them, but it's easier than doing it one-by-one in Twitter.
	DAY 6: Look at your follow queue in Tweetbig and continue to follow people. Look at your number of followers in TwitterGrader. Take a screenshot of this. You will use this to mark your progress by the end of 30 days.
	DAY 7: Create a profile picture that reflects positively on you and what you're focusing on. If you're focused on international business, get a clear and attractive headshot.
	DAY 8: Create a customized Twitter background. You can use one of the templates inside of ColourLovers,

I did it!	What to do
	which you can get to through the setup page on your Twitter profile.
	DAY 9: If you sincerely want to dominate Twitter, you'll make your own background. There are 120 pixels on the left, and people can view 500 pixels for your height.
	DAY 10: Make sure you put your picture in your Twitter background, as well as your website address, email, and other ways to engage with you, perhaps your LinkedIn profile address. Even if people can't click on the picture, it's good to show them you're on there.
	DAY 11: Make sure you fill out your profile with keywords for your niche. A singer might put in her influences (Nicki Minaj, Simon and Garfunkel) for example.
	DAY 12: Make sure you also put in a link to your website, and if you don't have a website yet, put a link to your LinkedIn profile. (Add your Twitter handle to your LinkedIn profile as well)
	DAY 13: Start retweeting the influencers in your niche. Go and comment on their articles, and then tweet that you commented, and what you thought of the article.
	DAY 14: Follow and mention influencers in your niche as well. If they are doing an event, even if it's far away from you, you can say, "Hey @wildwomanfund, wish I could be there!"
	DAY 15: When people start to follow you, mention them, say thank you, and ask them how you can help, or lead them back to your website.
	DAY 16: Keep track of your direct messages and make sure that you respond to people.
	DAY 17: Look at your followers and brainstorm, see if there's anyone in there you'd like to have a conversation with about your niche. Perhaps there's a way you two can connect, be blogging buddies, or

I did it!	What to do
	create a product together. You never know til you ask!
	DAY 18: Call someone from Twitter and have a conversation. If they are less experienced than you, listen carefully to their pain points, the things they complain about, and their language.
	DAY 19: Continue to schedule ten tweets per night in Hootsuite and link back to your witty blog posts, or to other unique and fascinating things you find about your niche. But if you retweet someone's tweet, don't just hit the retweet button. Say, "RT" and then copy paste their post, or say in 1 word what you think of it. Such as "Interesting: @flavie says 2012 is going to be a farce: http://bit.ly/Za"
	DAY 20: Write and schedule a series of tweets leading back to your blog posts addressing these pain points and specific language for your niche. Schedule tweets for the morning. Make 10 tweets about a post, and copy different sentences from the post.
	DAY 21: Make sure you have a blog post around this particular problem (or a series of posts about a series of problems) and use a URL shortener such as http://bit.ly to link back in your tweets. If you don't have them, write them.
	DAY 22: Start to create lists of your followers. When you start to list people, they will list you back, which makes you look more credible and popular, and helps you track various niches within your industry. For example if you're a tea fanatic, you might have a list just for tea shops you like, another for tea gurus, another for tea companies like Zhi tea.
	DAY 23: You can mention people you've listed that you've listed them. Like "I was happy to add @wildwomanfund to my "Fabulous Marketing Advice" list!
	DAY 24: Participate in hashtag conversations related to your niche, here's a list of over 400 chats: and see if you can get engaged in the discussions. If you don't know of any, @mention an influential person and ask

I did it!	What to do
	them if they know of any.
	DAY 25: With your new followers, message or mention them and ask if they'd like to do a Tweet chat with a hashtag specific to your niche (#dairyfarmers or #marketingprofs for example)
	DAY 26: Have your chat on the agreed upon time and direct message followers to ask friends to participate, give them something easy to tweet. Like "MarketingProfs chat today 1:00pm EST, #marketingprofs, let's talk about where our industry is going."
	DAY 27: Measuring your Progress: Watching your progress. Watch your stats and notice how many people are coming to your blog through Twitter or LinkedIn thanks to your cross posting.
	DAY 28: Watch your comments rise, and respond to comments. Continue to find and retweet people's articles on Twitter, and comment on the articles in Twitter.
	DAY 29: Watch your followers rise and continue to thank people publicly for following you and by mentioning them in your stream. Ask them questions. Be positive.
	DAY 30: Look at your stats in Tweetbig or TwitterGrader, the followers you had when you started, and the followers you have now. Pat yourself on the back for a job well done!

How do you work your Twitter Workflow, after you've done all of this?

1. Get on Twitter once a day and talk with people. Retweet people or comment on their posts.

2. Get on a chat at least once a week and talk with people.

3. List people, and try to have a phone call with someone from

Twitter at least once a month.

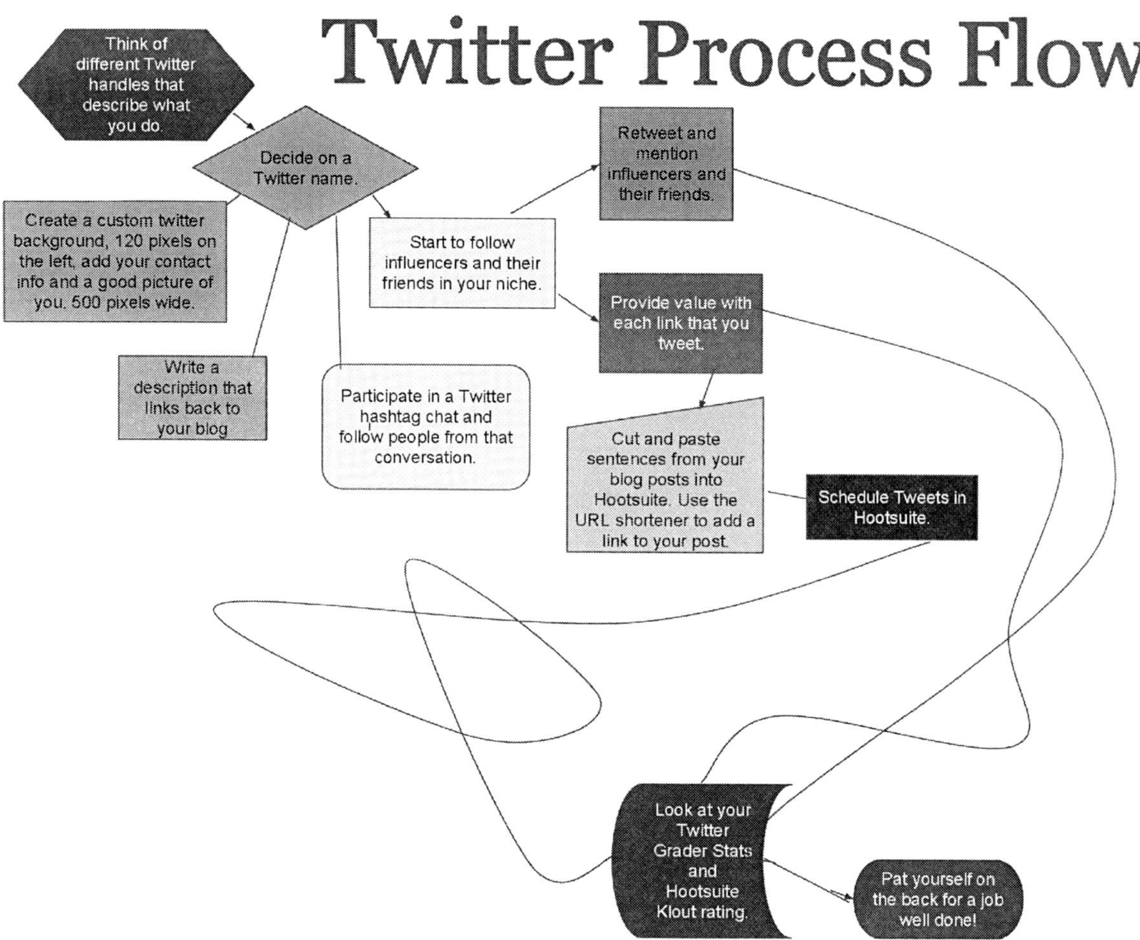
Twitter Process Flow
Think of different Twitter handles that describe what you do.
Decide on a Twitter name.
Create a custom twitter background, 120 pixels on the left, add your contact info and a good picture of you. 500 pixels wide.
Write a description that links back to your blog
Participate in a Twitter hashtag chat and follow people from that conversation.
Start to follow influencers and their friends in your niche.
Retweet and mention influencers and their friends.
Provide value with each link that you tweet.
Cut and paste sentences from your blog posts into Hootsuite. Use the URL shortener to add a link to your post.
Schedule Tweets in Hootsuite.
Look at your Twitter Grader Stats and Hootsuite Klout rating.
Pat yourself on the back for a job well done!

Commenting Worksheet

Commenting: How do you start conversations and continue the relationship online? And why would you want to?

Why should you comment? This has gotten me over 34,000 backlinks to date. This makes me come up a LOT in Google, without me spending any money on Google advertising.

How do you do this?

a. Identify blogs that allow comments, that write about what you care about.

b. Get Netvibes set up, and add the RSS feeds of these blogs.

What's Netvibes? It's a place where you can go to look at any search you've done, all in one place. So, for example, industry news, job searches, all of these searches can go in Netvibes. The Commenting Chapter goes into great detail about how to add feeds in Netvibes, with screenshots.

The green button that says "Add content" at the top is where you add the RSS feeds.

Once you've saved your first couple of feeds, think about categorizing them. There are tabs so you can separate your purposes, one for news, one for funny jokes, one for industry blogs, etc.

c. Commit to commenting on three to ten blogs per night, before you go to sleep, when you're too tired to do anything else.

d. Your comment strategy should be to provide your useful knowledge and opinion and a link back to your site or useful blog post. (Latter is better)

e. How can you tell that this is working? Download SEOBook for Firefox by going to http://seobook.com.

This sits in your browser, just below your bookmarks. You can instantly see how old a site is, how many incoming links a site has, what keywords they are using to drive traffic. You will see your incoming links go up. It's gratifying.

This sits right below your bookmarks and shows you how popular a particular page is.

f. A nice side benefit of commenting is that it gives you a LOT more material for blog posts.

What ideas do you have right now?

How Do you Automate Your Processes?

Since trying to use all of these tools all at once and keep track of everything all the time is a sure recipe for disaster, I am going to help you automate your processes.

Get on Hootsuite Http://Hootsuite.com

This is an incredibly useful tool for driving traffic to your website.

The main point of Hootsuite is the scheduling. It will automatically update your Twitter and LinkedIn and Facebook and any other pages for you. So you can set up updates weeks or months in advance, and just leave it. It's free for up to 5 accounts.

In Hootsuite you get stats on what your most popular tweets were, and more.

At the top you can see your different social networks. I have an art Twitter account, my main Twitter account, and my LinkedIn account. This is also where your Facebook icon would go, if you wanted to keep up a business Facebook page.

You have Pending Tweets on the left, Mentions in the middle, Retweets on the far right. You can also re-organize the order of these feeds any way you like.

You can track your stats by clicking on the little owl and seeing how many people have clicked on your links, and where in the world they were.

As of October 2012, Hootsuite is still free for up to 5 social networks. You may find this changes, but for personal use, it's still the tool of choice. It requires no download, unlike Tweetdeck, and you can customize it to fit your needs.

You can also use http://SocialOomph.com and http://su.pr
Feel free to try them all, and see which ones are easiest for you to use.

Getting more followers
Try http://TweetBig.com. It helps you gather Twitter followers and find influencers in your niche.

So the reason you want to do this is that it could take you several days or even weeks to find everyone on Twitter who cares about your niche. With this tool, you can search by name or by keyword, and get the attention of the influencers immediately, and learn who they are following too. This will save you so much time.

Find out what people are talking about
Use RSS feeds to track blogs that you want to comment on.

What are people saying about you?
Use a Google alert (see how to set up a Google Alert here: http://google.com/alerts), an RSS feed for whenever your name is mentioned, and/or http://socialmentionalert.com so that you can track when other people are talking about you, and respond to them, wherever they are.

What if you only have 15 minutes a day?

If you have 5 minutes a day

- Find one blog post and comment on it.
- Or find 5 influencers on Twitter to follow.

If you have 20 minutes a day
Make a blog post, and auto post it to Twitter

If you have 1 hour a day

- Make a blog post
- Go to 9.tc and create a shortened URL
- Post the URL in Hootsuite with different pithy sentences from the blog post 5-10 times.

If you have 90 minutes a day

- Make a blog post
- Go to 9.tc and create a shortened URL
- Post the URL in Hootsuite with different pithy sentences from the blog post 5-10 times.
- Comment on three to ten blogs linking back to your blog in a meaningful way.

30 Day Plan for Driving a LOT more Traffic to Your Website Checklist

I did it!	What to do
	DAY 1: Sign up for http://netvibes.com, play around with it. Make the background look like you want it to look. Set it up so it reflects YOU.
	DAY 2: Research different searches in your niche, set up Google alerts (if you don't know how, go to http://google.com/alerts to learn) or social mention alerts for keywords in your niche.
	DAY 3: Research blogs in your niche, using http://alltop.com, as well as Twitter influencers you follow, as well as using a Google search for bloggers in your niche.
	DAY 4: Figure out if these blogs are worth following by installing the http://SEOBook.com toolbar, which will show you how many incoming links they have. The more incoming links, the better.
	DAY 5: Add the blogs that seem to be influential to your Netvibes RSS reader. Put blogs for certain topics under their own tab. For example, if you're a fundraising blogger AND a philanthropy blogger, put these in two separate tabs. Also, make a tab for jokes. Because it's good to laugh as much as you can!
	DAY 6: If you've just started blogging, you may not have a lot of posts up yet, but looking at what people are talking about can give you ideas for posts. So start to make a little idea file of things you'd like to address or write a contrasting opinion to.
	DAY 7: Once you've read 3-4 blogs, see if you can find some RECENT articles you'd like to comment on. I'd say if the article is more than 1 week old, don't bother. Open up all of your blogs in tabs in your browser, and start to

I did it!	What to do
	comment. I like to comment at 10pm at night, when the rest of the work for the day is done.
	DAY 8: When you start to comment, don't just say "Nice post." Say, "Dear <name of blog writer> and then a thoughtful opinion on their post, whether agreeing or disagreeing. Sign off with "Sincerely" or another respectful sign off, and put your name at the bottom. And then if you are writing a long comment, consider copy-pasting your comment and making a whole blog post about it.
	DAY 9: Advanced: If you have a post related to the post that you are commenting on, say, "I would like to continue the conversation here: http://bit.ly/ty and link to your RELEVANT post.
	DAY 10: If you have time, comment on 10 blogs per night. Only comment on articles that are meaningful, interesting, or useful to you. Don't force yourself to comment on blogs that do not interest you. It will come across in the comment. Make sure you put your website under your name at the bottom of the comment. This will increase your incoming links.
	DAY 11: Now that you're comfortable commenting on blogs, I'd suggest that you start looking at article marketing. Create accounts at Hubspot, EzineArticles, and Squidoo today. Continue your commenting on blogs.
	DAY 12: Now you've created your accounts, search these places to see what has already been written about your field on here. If nothing has been written, you're in a good place to succeed. If something HAS been written, how can you put a new spin on this topic? Consider what pictures would go well with your topic. Consider what books you'd recommend people read. Gather your materials. Make a draft post.
	DAY 13: If you have a blog post about this topic, don't reuse it for the article marketing websites. They check and make sure that this post has not appeared elsewhere on the internet. So seriously. Don't do it. Write

I did it!	What to do
	something fresh and new. And you'll see that this will help you get traffic as well.
	DAY 14: If you want ideas on what you could write, 20 tips to run a fantastic promotional event, 5 ways to write the best resume, 22 ideas for blog posts on construction topics, etc.
	DAY 15: Look at what other people in your niche are writing about on the web. Could you give a new perspective? Talk about your experience? Talk about what you read in a book that was incorrect or a new way of doing something? Write 3-4 articles for your niche. Pick which ones you'll post in these 3 article marketing websites.
	DAY 16: What about the community that already exists on these websites? Start to comment on other people's related articles, start to click on their links, and ask them questions. If people have Twitter accounts, follow them on Twitter, and tweet about the article that they wrote.
	DAY 17: Make a point to visit the article marketing communities again, and see if you can find something to comment on.
	DAY 18: Turn one or two of your articles into pdfs, and add some more goodies, whether resources or pictures, and you might even want to invest in a graphic designer to design these. These are your first ebooks.
	DAY 19: Create an account on http://scribd.com. Upload your ebooks to Scribd, and charge something for them. If it's a short resource, I usually charge $5.00. Make sure that you make them un-printable, un-downloadable, un-embedable. And make sure if you're giving them a preview that you don't give away too much info. Just a taste. Just remember Scribd takes their cut, and you won't be able to take your money out until you reach $50.00.
	DAY 20: Now start to watch your stats rise every day that you make a new article, comment on a blog, or upload a new Scribd document.

I did it!	What to do
	DAY 21: Embed one of your Scribd documents into your website, either at the end of a relevant blog post, or a resource page. This will help even more people buy your work.
	DAY 22: Check and see if there have been any comments on your articles.
	DAY 23: Look at some of the most popular articles in your niche, and write your own spin on the subject. For example, "5 successful event planning tips" could become "10 things to avoid when planning your event."
	DAY 24: Get on http://Tweetbig.com and find the influencers in your niche. Also do a keyword search for your keywords. Start using Tweetbig and connecting with influential Twitterers, mentioning them, retweeting them, and soon they will start mentioning you as well. This can lead to more followers for you and more traffic back to your website.
	DAY 25: Get on Twitter and set up an alert for anytime someone mentions your keyword in your area, and see if you can be of use to these people, either leading them to an article you've written that can solve their problem, or asking them if you can write a blog post on how to solve their problem. This is especially good for local small businesses. People will be impressed that you were listening, but didn't try to sell them your services.
	DAY 26: Keep track of where most of your search traffic is coming from with Google Analytics and write a post on this topic, or even create an ebook specialized to the topic people are searching for when they find your site, and make it part of the free gift they get for signing up for your e-newsletter.
	DAY 27: Take part in a Twitter Chat related to your niche and offer one of your articles as a resource for the discussion, if appropriate. But mainly just listen and compliment people on their good ideas. You can find a whole list of Twitter chats here: http://bit.ly/TwitterChatMaster
	DAY 28: Go back and connect with the people you met

I did it!	What to do
	on Twitter chat and say thank you for talking with me, I'm following you now, and would love to talk more about your areas of expertise. Want to have a phone call? And you would not believe the tremendous opportunities that arise just from talking on the phone with people you meet from Twitter. (For more info on this, check out *The Tao of Twitter* by Mark Schaefer)
	DAY 29: Tweet about your blog posts and Scribd documents with Hootsuite. Use the URL shortener **http://bit.ly**.
	DAY 30: Enter your website into Press release website directories such as Pingomatic, so that every time you post, people can be kept updated. Also, make sure you've got an RSS feed for your site (if you have Wordpress, you already do). Then step back & celebrate, pat yourself on the back for a job well done!

Advanced Social Media Workflow: What to do daily, weekly & monthly

How do you manage your Social Media Work Flow?

Daily
Twitter Workflow: Get on Twitter once a day and talk with people. Retweet people or comment on their posts.

Blog Workflow: Monitor comments and questions, if you publish a post, track who retweets or mentions it on Twitter.

LinkedIn Workflow: Check and see if you have messages, see who has looked at your profile/group comments/posts.

Weekly
Twitter Workflow: Get on a Twitter chat at least once a week and talk with people.

Blog Workflow: Write one to five blog posts per week, comment on three to ten blogs per night.

LinkedIn Workflow: Sign up for groups and participate.

Monthly
Twitter Workflow: List people on Twitter, and try to have a phone call with someone from Twitter at least once a month.

Blog Workflow: Track how many visitors you got, make sure you guest post at least once, and have someone guest post for you, or interview someone.

LinkedIn Workflow: Give and get one recommendation.

Track Your Progress with Metrics

How do you report your progress to your boss? Which metrics matter?

What matters in the first 6-12 months is how much you are touching others. How you are getting the word out about your services or products.

So important metrics are your reach on Facebook, Twitter, LinkedIn, YouTube via views, likes, followers, tweets and retweets, as well as how many people click through to your website, sign up for your e-newsletter, or buy your products.

I've created metrics worksheets on the next few pages so that when people ask you: "But what have you REALLY accomplished in the last month or quarter?"

You can show them how month after month, you have added more views, sales, likes, followers, e-newsletter signups, and more. Feel free to photocopy these worksheets to use over and over again.

LinkedIn Metrics Worksheet

LinkedIn Metrics	Month:	Month:	Month:	Month:
# of Comments				
# of Profile views				
# of People joining your group				
# of groups you actively participate in.				
Traffic to your website from LinkedIn (use special URL)				

LinkedIn Metrics	Month:	Month:	Month:	Month:
# of Comments				
# of Profile views				
# of People joining your group				
# of groups you actively participate in.				
Traffic to your website from LinkedIn (use special URL)				

LinkedIn Metrics	Month:	Month:	Month:	Month:

# of Comments				
# of Profile views				
# of People joining your group				
# of groups you actively participate in.				
Traffic to your website from LinkedIn (use special URL)				

Twitter Metrics Worksheet

Twitter Metrics	Month:	Month:	Month:	Month:
# of @mentions				
# of times you tweet a blog post in different ways.				
# Chats participated in				
# of new followers				
# of retweets				
# of lists				
Traffic to your website from Twitter				
# of Calls with new Twitter friends				
Answers to Twitter survey				
Follow up from Twitter survey answers				

Twitter Metrics	Month:	Month:	Month:	Month:
# of @mentions				
# of times you tweet a blog post in different ways.				
# Chats participated in				
# of new followers				
# of retweets				
# of lists				

Traffic to your website from Twitter				
# of Calls with new Twitter friends				
Answers to Twitter survey				
Follow up from Twitter survey answers				

Twitter Metrics	Month:	Month:	Month:	Month:
# of @mentions				
# of times you tweet a blog post in different ways.				
# Chats participated in				
# of new followers				
# of retweets				
# of lists				
Traffic to your website from Twitter				
# of Calls with new Twitter friends				
Answers to Twitter survey				
Follow up from Twitter survey answers				

Website Metrics Worksheet

Website Metrics	Month:	Month:	Month:	Month:
# of Visits				
# of Uniques				
# of visitors from Twitter (Create a twitter landing page on your site)				
# of comments				
# of Pages				
# of visits on your sales page				
# of realtime chats with visitors				
# of e-newsletter signups				
% of e-newsletter opens				
% of e-newsletter clicks				
# of sales from website				

Website Metrics	Month:	Month:	Month:	Month:
# of Visits				
# of Uniques				
# of visitors from Twitter				
# of comments				
# of Pages				

# of visits on your sales page				
# of realtime chats with visitors				
# of e-newsletter signups				
% of e-newsletter opens				
% of e-newsletter clicks				
# of sales from website				

Website Metrics	Month:	Month:	Month:	Month:
# of Visits				
# of Uniques				
# of visitors from Twitter				
# of comments				
# of Pages				
# of visits on your sales page				
# of realtime chats with visitors				
# of e-newsletter signups				
% of e-newsletter opens				
% of e-newsletter clicks				
# of sales from website				

Misc Metrics Worksheet

Misc Metrics	Month:	Month:	Month:	Month:
Put your presentations out through				
Slideshare # of views				
Scribd # of reads				
LinkedIn # of views				
Other # of views				
# of presentations I did, giving or receiving.				
# of relevant blog comments I did.				
# of guest posts I did				
# of incoming links, according to MajesticSEO				

Misc Metrics	Month:	Month:	Month:	Month:
Put your presentations out through				
Slideshare # of views				
Scribd # of reads				
LinkedIn # of views				
Other # of views				

# of presentations I did, giving or receiving.				
# of relevant blog comments I did.				
# of guest posts I did				
# of incoming links, according to MajesticSEO				

Misc Metrics	Month:	Month:	Month:	Month:
Put your presentations out through				
Slideshare # of views				
Scribd # of reads				
LinkedIn # of views				
Other # of views				
# of presentations I did, giving or receiving.				
# of relevant blog comments I did.				
# of guest posts I did				
# of incoming links, according to MajesticSEO				

Sales Metrics Worksheet

Sales Metrics	Month:	Month:	Month:	Month:
E-newsletter signups				
E-newsletter click-through rates				
E-newsletter open rates				
E-newsletter unsubscribes				
Queries for services				
Queries for speaking				
Donations				
Sales of tickets				
Sales of ebooks				
Sales of services				
Other:				

Sales Metrics	Month:	Month:	Month:	Month:
E-newsletter signups				
E-newsletter click-through rates				
E-newsletter open rates				
E-newsletter unsubscribes				

Queries for services				
Queries for speaking				
Donations				
Sales of tickets				
Sales of ebooks				
Sales of services				
Other:				

Sales Metrics	Month:	Month:	Month:	Month:
E-newsletter signups				
E-newsletter click-through rates				
E-newsletter open rates				
E-newsletter unsubscribes				
Queries for services				
Queries for speaking				
Donations				
Sales of tickets				
Sales of ebooks				
Sales of services				
Other:				

Tool rankings

These tools are ranked in order of usefulness, of information they provide, not in order of cost, or ease of installation or use. No endorsement is implied and no money is changing hands here.
5 is best, 1 is worst.

Metric Tools	Ranked
Twitter Metric Tools	
SproutSocial: This will give you demographic information about your followers on LinkedIn, Twitter and Facebook. Useful. http://sproutsocial.com	5
TwitSprout: This has cute graphics for the rate you are gaining or losing followers, but now with so many follow spammers on Twitter, it's less useful. It will also show you how often you tweet in graph form. http://twitsprout.com	3
TweetPsych: This tool will show you how much you tweet about certain things, you can also look up other people. It's interesting though not directly related to sales. http://tweetpsych.com	3
TwitterGrader: This is a tool from Hubspot measuring the effectiveness of your Twitter account, if it's growing, etc. Similar to TwitSprout but not as beautiful. Http://tweet.grader.com	2
TweetReach: This tool is useful to show your boss how many potential people viewed your tweets. Much like newspapers and billboards will promise potential eyeballs. http://tweetreach.com	5
Your website	Ranked

Google Analytics: I like how Google analytics will show you where people click on your page, but I find the rest of their metrics needlessly complicated.	3
Hubspot Marketing Grader: This will measure if you've got page descriptions, if you have a lot of backlinks, if you have a conversion form on your site, if you have Twitter integrated with your site, how many retweets on average a post has, etc. Useful. http://marketing.grader.com	4
SEOBook: This will show you the number of incoming links to your website via Yahoo search, Majestic SEO, and SEOmoz. It will also show you the number of incoming links to OTHER websites, which is useful when considering where you should guest post. Http://seobook.com	5
Finding New Customers Tools	Ranked
Twellow: This is more of a yellow pages site, not updated in real time. http://twellow.com	4
Who's On: This tool will show you who is on your website and let you chat with them in real-time. http://whoson.com	5
KissMetrics/KissInsight will let you do a popup poll for website visitors to see if they are finding what they needed. http://kissmetrics.com	3
TweetBig: This will help you build targeted followers fast. It will also show you who is the most influential of your current followers, who follows back, as well as sets up automated tweets for you if you want. http://tweetbig.com	5
Managing Workflow Tools	
Hootsuite.com: I love this tool because you can manage multiple social platforms there, such as Twitter, Facebook, LinkedIn, and you can schedule tweets, keep track of mentions, DMs, and your stream, all on one screen, unlike on Twitter. http://hootsuite.com	5

Peoplebrowsr.com: This is useful for sentiment analysis, as well as figuring out how many people you reached. Similar to SproutSocial. Http://peoplebrowsr.com	4
What are some tools YOU use? Put them here.	

Advanced: Tracking Metrics on your Site	Ranked
Whos.Amung.Us: You can see the # of people on your site with a little side widget. http://whos.amung.us	
Lijit: Tracks audience data http://lijit.com	
VisualWebsiteOptimizer: For A/B testing of your website elements http://visualwebsiteoptimizer.com	
Optomizely: For A/B Testing of your website	
Tynt.com: See what people are copy-pasting from your website. http://tynt.com	5

Now that you can see all of the ways people track you online, and if you'd like to KEEP people from tracking you online, do the next worksheet.

Be More Anonymous Online Worksheets

Browse the Internet More Anonymously Tasks	**Done?**
Do not use Internet Explorer. Use Firefox or Opera.	
Use Firefox Stylish Add-ons & Plugins: Find these for ad blocking on various websites incl. Gmail, yahoo, hotmail, livejournal, huffingtonpost, nytimes, Facebook, Hootsuite promoted tweets, and others.	
Do not use Google to search online. Use http://DuckDuckGo.com. This search engine does not collect personal information about you.	
Install Aries Cookie Block Plugin for Firefox. This will help stop advertisers from tracking which websites you visited, and in what order.	
Adblock Plus: Will block ads on Firefox and Opera	
Ghostery: Will block tracking software on any website unless you tell it not to.	
Bookmark the places you go regularly, and then auto-clear your browsing history & cookies every time you close your browser. And disable third-party cookies. This means you have to retype your password each time, but sites will not be able to track you as easily, and your privacy is worth that little inconvenience.	
If you don't believe anonymity is necessary, install Collusion, a Firefox browser plugin, to see how websites try to track you if you don't have the above plugins installed.	
If you must use Gmail or Google+, log out of these services before using Google to search, or before you watch a YouTube video. Otherwise Google will track your viewing history and use your information to sell to advertisers.	

LinkedIn Privacy Checklist

Be More Anonymous on LinkedIn Tasks	**Done?**
Do not reveal the dates you went to high school or college.	
After 5 years, do not have a date that you worked somewhere. You can list places you've worked in your summary instead.	
Do not disclose your birth date on your LinkedIn profile.	
Make your profile and connections only fully visible to your connections by going to your settings page.	
Do not make your contact information available to anyone. You can control this on the settings page.	
Do not connect with people you don't know. If a stranger wants to connect with you, ignore them or report them as spam. If you've already connected with strangers, disconnect with them by going to your "contacts page" and then click "remove connections" on the mid-top right of that page.	
Opt out of LinkedIn advertisement emails & sharing with 3rd party networks. Go to your settings page and make sure that you get those advertisements out of your inbox.	
Make your public profile as anonymous as possible. Go to settings, then go to account and "edit your public profile" and uncheck most of the information there.	
Read http://tos-dr.info to make sure you understand what privacy you are giving up by being on LinkedIn.	
BONUS: To stop LinkedIn Ads, use Firefox Stylish Add-on plugin.	
BONUS: To stop LinkedIn ad networks from tracking you, use Ghostery Firefox Add-on.	

Twitter Privacy Checklist

Use Twitter More Anonymously Tasks	Done?
Do not use a location sharing service such as 4Square or another site where you "check-in" your location. This allows people to see where you are, what you're doing, and how often you go to this place. If someone were planning to rob you, then your Twitter account would be the first place they could look to see where you were and when you would be likely to come home.	
Do not put in your real location in your Twitter profile	
Tweet primarily about professional topics, not personal ones.	
Read http://tos-dr.info to make sure you understand what privacy you are giving up.	
Go to your Settings page and Opt out of Twitter advertisement emails & sharing with 3rd party networks.	

Facebook Privacy

You can set your Facebook profile to "private" but the matter at hand is simply one of trust. Facebook has had many breaches of privacy over the last several years, including resetting your profile privacy settings without your permission[*], resetting your address book in your phone for your "Facebook" email address[**], a 2012 partnership with a company called Datalogix that ties your Facebook profile with your purchases[***] and more.

In order to protect your privacy, I would say simply, don't use Facebook.

Google & Google+ Privacy

* http://www.business2community.com/facebook/warning-your-facebook-privacy-settings-have-been-reset-065965

** http://gizmodo.com/5922836/is-the-facebook-email-fiasco-worse-than-we-all-thought

***http://www.cbc.ca/news/technology/story/2012/09/25/f-facebook-privacy-list.html

There are so many things wrong with using Google products when it comes to privacy. And there has been much criticism of Google, Google+ and other Google products[****] over the last several years.

Here are just a few. Google reading your Gmail emails and giving you ads related to what you're writing about[*****]. Google noticing that you're logged into your Gmail or Google+ account and giving you search results based on who you know. I don't know about you, but when I go online, I want to see search results based on who I don't know. Google tying your YouTube views to your Gmail account, to get an even more accurate picture of the kind of consumer you are.

If you think you need to be on Google+, I assure you, people don't make buying decisions on Google+. They don't look for new partnerships there either.

If you're concerned about privacy when you browse the internet, use http://DuckDuckGo.com instead.

Note: With Google's 2012 "privacy" policy and Facebook's "privacy" policy you are better off not using Gmail or Facebook if you want a modicum of privacy online. Use a mail client like Thunderbird on your desktop instead.

****http://en.wikipedia.org/wiki/Criticism_of_Google
*****http://privacyrights.org/ar/GmailLetter.htm

End Note

Thank you for being brave enough to start this journey. Feel free to make a note in the last few pages of this book. This is YOUR book. Let it be your guide. Track your progress and don't be afraid to email me with questions.

I want you to know that I am proud of you for taking control of your reputation, and figuring out how to create more sources of income/relationships/kudos for yourself, your business or your nonprofit.

If you need any help along the way, I am here for you. You can email me at info@wildsocialmedia.com. You can say hi to me on Twitter at @wildwomanfund

If you'd like bulk books or a presentation to your company or group, feel free to let me know via the methods above.

You can also reach out to me on http://wildsocialmedia.com.

You are the best, and I know you can do it! It may seem like a lot of work, but the work pays off, and you'll have built relationships that can sustain your nonprofit or business for years to come.

Mazarine Treyz

Mazarine Treyz

About the author Mazarine Treyz

Mazarine helps businesses get more customers and more cash through online marketing. She also helps nonprofits get more donors.

Since 1999, she has written online. Mazarine brings over a decade of experience to online marketing. In her personalized presentations, Mazarine helps people measure social media's impact, convince the boss, come up with new ways to get more out of your social media efforts, figure out what's working to drive customer and donor behavior, and more.

Ms. Treyz has presented for the City of Austin, Oregon Association of Minority Entrepreneurs and the City of Portland, Big Austin, a micro enterprise incubator, as well as at the Scleroderma Foundation National Leadership Conference, Meals on Wheels national webinars, and many others.

Mazarine's presentations have helped clients get featured in major media outlets resulting in thousands in sales and donations, increased attendance at events, increased sales, newsletter subscribers, exposure, affiliate sales, students for teachers, and more. With hands-on, how-to instructions, Mazarine can help your team bring in more customers and more cash for your business.

Visit http://MazarineTreyz.com for more information on hiring Mazarine for your next conference, training or webinar. Bulk discounts of this book are available.

What people are saying about Mazarine Treyz's Presentations

"Since taking Mazarine's e-newsletter webinar, my open rate has jumped from 8% to 14%!" -Kenita Pierce-Lewis, H.O.P.E. Inc. Georgia

Excellent presentation, helpful, informative, and motivating! -John Panarese, Executive Director, Animal Rescue League of Fall River, MA"

"Your presentation gave me many fresh ideas that I would like to incorporate into my upcoming mailings. I plan to review my notes and the supplemental materials provided in order to create an "action plan" for the lessons learned. Thank you!" -Amanda Parker, Grants and Development Manager, OPERA America

"Mazarine's webinar gave me TONS of ideas for making our mailing more effective. The opportunity for questions and answers was also extremely valuable! Thanks!" —T.J. Holsen, Development Director, Parents as Teachers of Lake County, Inc. Indiana

"We are a grassroots organization doing our fifth fundraising event next year. Mazarine's webinar helped us brainstorm who to approach and lots of ways to convince them to sponsor us! Tremendous value! " -Denise Hawkinson, PhD., Board member, Post-Partum Health Alliance

"I was highly impressed with Mazarine's presentation. She provides practical advice and pertinent information on best practices, how-to strategies and more." -Karrie Groves Riemer, Operation Sack Lunch, Seattle, WA

"Mazarine's workshop helped me 'think big' for a big event. Great resources, fresh ideas and lots of energy. Thank you!" -Leigh Crow, Director, Resource Development, United Way of Forsyth County, Georgia

"I learned so much from Mazarine's seminar! I have already put some of her tips into place with great success! It's definitely a valuable presentation." -Colleen Payne, Executive Director, Spinal Bifida Association of Kentucky

Book Mazarine Treyz to speak at your event or in a custom webinar for your company or organization. http://wildsocialmedia.com/contact

Notes

Notes